CAROL VORDERMAN'S

SUMMER DETOX

THE 14 DAY MINI DETOX

Carol Vorderman with Anita Bean

TED SMART

CHECK WITH YOUR DOCTOR

Before starting this or any other detox diet programme, you should consult your doctor. In particular this should be done with regard to any allergies you have to any of the foods, drinks, products, supplements or other recommendations contained in this programme. The detox diet may not be suitable for everyone. Pregnant women should be especially careful and ensure that their doctor advises that the detox diet is suitable for them. If you are taking medication or have any medical condition, you should check with your doctor first.

While the authors have made every effort to ensure that the information contained in this book is as accurate and up to date as possible, it is advisory only and should not be used as an alternative to seeking specialist medical advice. The authors and publishers cannot be held responsible for actions that may be taken by a reader as a result of reliance on the information contained in this book, which are taken entirely at the reader's own risk.

Dedication

To everyone who worked on this book.
And to the thousands of people who followed the detox and let me know how much it has changed their lives.

Carol Vorderman

Carol Vorderman
Sole Worldwide Representation
John Miles Organisation
Fax: 01275 810186
Email: john@johnmiles.org.uk

Carol Vorderman was assisted in the writing of this book by **Anita Bean** BSc, a nutritionist, magazine columnist and author of six top-selling books on food and nutrition.

This edition produced for
The Book People Ltd, Hall Wood Avenue
Haydock St Helens, WA11 9UL

A catalogue record for the book is available from the British Library.

ISBN 0 7535 0815X

All photographs of Carol Vorderman by Karl Grant
Designed by Smith & Gilmour
Printed and bound in Great Britain by The Bath Press, CPI Group

CONTENTS

CHAPTER 1
INTRODUCTION

Summer is fantastic. When the first days of summer come along and the sun beats down, it beams a gladness into your heart and puts a smile upon your face. Summer can be a magical time of year: the late evening light; sitting outside to eat and chat; doing nothing in the garden all day; switching off the central heating at long last.

And now with package holidays and constant special offers, we go in search of the summer sun all year round. Millions go away for their hols, not just in July and August, but in the midst of winter too. We may not live in sunny climes but we sure as hell enjoy them while we're there. And so we should.

One of the best things about summer is casting off the heavy coats and hats, losing the woolly tights and polo-neck jumpers and feeling the sun against your skin. Gorgeous. And that's what you want to be: downright gorgeous, wearing gorgeous clothes and gorgeous shoes with gorgeous skin.

But sometimes it's just not that easy is it? All the brochures full of people prancing along the beach looking happy and free. 'Give me some of that,' you cry. So you book it, and you get the suitcase out. But what do you fill the suitcase with? Which of last year's clothes still fit? You take all your kit off, look at yourself in the mirror and, 'Aaaaaaagh'. What is this greying blobby mass staring back at you?

Summer means there are no more places to hide, no more boots and scarves and long-sleeved jumpers to cover the bumps. There's no escape. Try on the vests and the shorts and the skirts and what pokes out? Miserable looking skin, with some dimply bits which weren't there last year? Where the hell did they come from? It's not fair but it's true and as you get older it gets even harder to hide it all. It's happened to me often enough – hell, it's happened to all of us. But with this 14-day

mini detox and a little bit of time left before you dash off, between us we can change what you see in the mirror. OK, realistically in 14 days, what changes are you after before you check in at the airport:
Lose bloat
Lose weight
Kill off some of the cellulite
Feel healthier
Feel fitter
Get great skin, shiny hair and sparkling eyes?

Well, it's possible with this 14-day mini detox.

Over the last four years, I've become an absolute believer in the detox diet. It differs from all the other diets I've tried before. Here are the facts:
I'm 42 (although I might start lying about it soon)
I don't weigh myself
I don't count calories
I don't go to a gym

BUT
I'm a size 8 to 10
My weight has stayed steady for four years
I've bags of energy
My skin is good
I feel healthier and younger
I eat loads of food every day

You might be aware of the *Detox for Life* 28-day diet book which has become a bestseller. I first followed that diet four years ago and it changed my weight and my attitude to food forever. I used to think that weight control was about counting calories and denying myself foods which I wanted to eat. I don't believe that now.

I'm just over 5' 6" tall and from my mid-20s I was always a dress size larger than I wanted to be, but somehow I could never shift the inches and the pounds. I knew how many calories were in everything in the supermarket, but it didn't stop me from eating the bad stuff. Like most women, getting on the scales in the morning could depress me for the rest of the day. For years I couldn't kick the habits. I've half-heartedly tried just about every eating plan invented over the years. I'd find out about some magic cabbage diet, try it for three days, get fed up, go back to eating the old stuff, lose two pounds then put four back on. With this yo-yo dieting I stayed at about a size 12, which was OK but I wasn't happy with the way I ate: I felt guilty a lot of the time.

But it was when I had my first baby that my weight started to get out of control. I was constantly tired and I couldn't lose the excess weight after I'd had Katie. I went up to a size 14 and felt old. After three years, I decided to do something radical and started going to the gym with a personal trainer four times a week. It cost a fortune and a lot of effort but it was worth it in the end. I was fit for a while and soon after got pregnant for a second time. I was 36 when I had Cameron. This time I didn't put on as much weight. I was a size 12 after he was born but I still wanted to lose some inches.

And so four years ago I tried my first detox. A friend of mine had been on a detox diet and, when I saw her, her skin was beautiful and she looked better than she had for years. That made up my mind. After a week on the detox, I had headaches and didn't feel too good but I kept to the plan for a month, although I wasn't very strict about it. By the end of that month I'd dropped a dress size, had so much energy I was even more irritating than I normally am, and had altered the way I ate forever.

After the first 28 days were over, I came off the diet but I found that for the next 6 months I ate very well because I wanted to. I found that I wanted to eat fruit and vegetables and rice and pulses – it was my choice. I added a lot of fish, chicken, tea and milk – and alcohol, of course – to my diet, but magically the weight stayed off. After six months, I decided to try another 28 days on the detox plan and that time I stuck to it quite rigidly because I knew I would gain great results. I dropped another dress size and felt better still. But it wasn't just about weight. My cellulite diminished dramatically, my skin was smoother than it had ever been, and I felt 'alive'. And remember, all this happened without counting calories or going to the gym.

In all the years since, I have probably only fluctuated by half a dress size, the equivalent of maybe 5 pounds, though I'm not sure of the exact weight because I don't weigh myself anymore. I eat out a lot, I have bad months of chocolate and pasta, big breakfasts in bed, Christmases which last for weeks and yet, somehow, the weight stays off because the detox has become ingrained in how I want to eat. When I've binged for a week, I don't want to do it anymore. My body tells me to stop, not my brain. It tells me it's lacking in the good stuff. I thought only prissy little misses with neat little figures who iron their knickers ate properly, but I'm a complete convert to how following the detox once or twice a year can change the way you eat forever, without you having to become a boring pain in the neck.

I am also now a believer that it is the quality of the food you put inside your body, and not the quantity, which matters. It's not about calories, endlessly counting your low-fat biscuits, or keeping your calorie count low by only eating three bars of chocolate in a day and nothing else. That's just nonsense. I've tried that and it didn't change how I ate in the long term. It doesn't retrain your body to want the good things. The detox does. I know. It's been four years now and it hasn't failed.

But don't just take my work for it. Since releasing *Detox for Life*, I've been stopped in the street by men and women who are thrilled with the results they've achieved. People who've lost stones in weight and feel younger and healthier than they have for years. Men who say that it has transformed the women in their lives and so they're now trying it for themselves. Famous people; nurses; mothers; bankers; men and women of all ages. They have all discovered how the detox can change their life.

After the couple of 28-day plans during my first year of eating well, I've followed a mini detox for 14 days twice a year, particularly just before a holiday. I found that I didn't need to follow the strict 28-day diet and only needed a shorter boost. In 14 days on the mini detox I can lose quite a few inches of bloat and gain a much better complexion all over. It can make such a big difference, and the mini detox is always easier to follow in the summer months. Somehow when the sun shines, you fancy a salad for lunch. That's why I've brought out this mini detox diet with new recipes written for the summer months, full of smoothies and fresh flavours.

Because this is a shorter eating plan (only 14 days instead of 28), the harder you try, the better your result will be. As well as following the eating plan, it's very important to treat your skin well too. You must brush your whole body at least once a day with a dry-skin brush or loofah (I prefer the brush). The difference in your skin texture will be enormous after two weeks, and your skin will honestly feel as soft as a baby's bum. Keep brushing and you won't have a problem with throwing your tights back in the drawer and baring your legs.

And if you've left a little more time before your holiday and you're happy with the results of the mini detox, then you can carry on with this eating plan for a full 28 days. It will do you the world of good and you will never look back.

This mini detox is about eating good things that your body finds easier to digest. Foods that feed your skin. It is about positive things that you find happening to your body. Your shape changes; your eyes sparkle; your skin glows; you sleep better; you take fewer medicines; you feel alive when you wake up in the morning. You feel ready for the summer.

If you stick to the mini detox then this is what will happen to you:
You will lose inches
You will feel alive and energetic
Your skin will improve dramatically
You will enjoy the summer more.

Wherever you're going, or even if you've decided to stay at home, have a great summer, enjoy the sun, and smile inside and out.

Happy holidays.

Carol Vorderman

CHAPTER 2
REAL SUCCESS

Celia Lyons, 47, former A & E senior nurse and mother of two children

'My weight had gradually crept up. I wasn't really aware of how much bigger I had become until one day I realised I no longer fitted comfortably into my size 14 clothes. I certainly didn't want to buy a new wardrobe of larger sizes! I felt lethargic and fed up. That's when I knew I had to do something about my diet.

Carol Vorderman's Detox for Life appealed to me because it emphasises wellbeing rather than weight loss. Carol is a terrific role model because she looks amazing and has bags of energy. I thought: "If Carol can look that good, then so can I!" I was ready to follow in her footsteps.

The detox diet was surprisingly easy to follow. Far from being restrictive and boring, it is really varied and full of delicious food. Although I had to give up a few old favourites – chocolates, Danish pastries, etc. – the meals and snacks were so tasty that I didn't feel deprived. Most of all, I enjoyed the salads, which were wonderful and really quick to make. I shared these with the rest of my family – topping up their plate with fish- or meat-based dishes. My children are now great salad fans!

My favourite quick meals were the dips with crudités, stir-fries and chickpea salads. I often used bags of ready-washed salad leaves then added extra vegetables. One of the biggest changes I made was drinking lots more water than before. That seemed to make me feel much more energetic.

After 14 days, I felt full of life. I no longer felt tired in the afternoons and evenings. It was as if I had revved up a few gears. I quite literally buzzed around all day doing all my chores – and with energy to spare! I can now fit so much more into my day.

As a bonus, I lost half a stone in 14 days. I continued to eat healthily beyond 14 days, keeping to the main principles of the detox but allowing myself just a few extras. My clothes feel much more comfortable. I love it when people remark how well I look and want me to let them in on my secret! I know the diet has made me look and feel a lot younger.'

Tracey Martin, 35, airline passenger services agent and mother of one

'Having booked a holiday in the sun was a huge incentive for me to lose some weight. I wanted to look good by the poolside and have enough energy to join in the nightlife. I didn't want to be the one covering up in baggy clothes during the daytime nor flagging early in the evening.

Apart from being overweight, I was also feeling lethargic, sluggish and bloated. Not the ideal way to feel before a holiday! The first thing I did was visit the supermarket armed with a healthy shopping list. I felt so proud loading up my trolley with loads of fruit, vegetables and nuts … and skipping the aisles full of biscuits and chocolates.

The biggest change I made was eating a healthy breakfast: muesli, porridge or prunes with natural yoghurt. Previously, I would skip breakfast – especially if I was working an early shift – but I would 'pick' later on in the day and almost certainly end up eating more calories. On the detox diet, I made sure that I ate regularly. I focused on looking after myself properly and stopped snacking on biscuits.

Weekends used to be my big downfall, as I treated myself to apple pies and other sweet snacks. Now I make sure that I have a supply of fresh fruit in the house and ban those sweet foods from my shopping trolley. Perhaps the hardest habit to break was my evening cup of tea with a biscuit. The first few days without them were hard but now I honestly don't miss them.

My favourite foods on the *Summer Detox* were the smoothies – I loved the strawberry and mango smoothie and Supercharge. They are such an easy way to get extra fruit into my diet and they really do taste delicious. I also added a squeeze of lemon juice to salads and vegetables and would sprinkle over sesame seeds or chopped walnuts to make them more interesting. In fact, I have developed quite a passion for coleslaw and the rocket and watercress salad.

During the *Summer Detox*, I continued to exercise three times a week – aqua aerobics or legs, bums and tums classes – which really made me feel good about myself. Although I wasn't a heavy smoker, I managed to stop smoking during the second week and can honestly say that I haven't missed having a cigarette since.

I have lost 5 pounds in 14 days. I now feel much more energetic and my clothes feel looser. Amazingly, my PMS symptoms have practically vanished and I didn't have any of the usual food cravings. My skin feels and looks smoother. My eyes are sparkling and even my teeth feel cleaner! I can't wait to get on that aeroplane!'

Mary Hamilton, 41, classroom assistant and mother of two children

'I wanted the *Summer Detox* to kick-start a healthier way of eating and living. I was fed up feeling bloated and sluggish. I had no energy, I felt tired all the time and, as a result, I was often short-tempered with the children. I wanted to be able to keep up with my children, and feel proud that I could combine being a single parent with a demanding job. I didn't want to be fat, frumpy and 41! I knew that I had to change the way I ate for the sake of my family as well as my health.

I felt that I could manage 14 days of detox eating; after all a fortnight didn't seem too daunting if I were to end up feeling hungry! But I need not have worried. I loved the meals, I never went hungry and quickly became a real convert to stir-fries and salads. During the *Summer Detox* I shared the recipes with my partner and the children. I simply added an extra main course – say fish or a meat dish – to the vegetable dish for the other family members. My favourite recipes were the hummus, muesli, stir-fried summer vegetables and the summer risotto with spinach. Even my children grew to love the crunchy stir-fried vegetables. I would make a large batch of hummus and take a small pot to work with some crudités or a tub of salad.

I bought a juicer, which was one of my best investments. I used it almost daily to make delicious juices. Even now I often take some fresh juice to work in an insulated flask. It really does make me feel satisfied and full of energy during the day. I carried a bottle of water around with me, too, to make sure that I didn't get dehydrated.

I stopped drinking coffee and tea and soon realised that I was sleeping much better for it. I was finally able to "switch off" at night, fall asleep quickly and then wake up in the morning feeling refreshed! That's something I hadn't been able to do for a long time!

The hardest things to give up were cheese and wine. Before the *Summer Detox*, I would eat a lot of cheese and drink a couple of glasses of wine most evenings but now I realise that those things were simply habits.

After following the *Summer Detox* I felt fit, healthy and full of renewed optimism. My skin is smoother and, as a bonus, I have lost 3 pounds. The *Summer Detox* has also kick-started a new exercise habit for me. I have taken up yoga, which has helped my back problem and reduced my stress levels. I have stuck to most of the detox principles – avoiding dairy, salt and fatty foods – purely because I feel so much better for it. It's great not feeling tired and depressed any more.'

CHAPTER 3
THE HEALTH AND DIET CHALLENGE

Has winter left you feeling lethargic, sluggish and a few pounds heavier than you'd like? Do you have a niggling suspicion that you haven't been eating as well as you ought to? Are you unhappy with your weight or worried about your health? Well, now is the perfect time to take stock of your health. Welcome to the health and diet challenge.

Ever noticed how you seem to come down with a cold or infection when your diet hasn't been up to scratch? Or how eating mostly processed salty or sugary foods for just one day quickly robs you of energy and vigour? Do that for a while and your skin soon loses its glow, your eyes look dull and your hair stops looking shiny. There's no doubt that what you eat makes a huge difference to the way you feel, the amount of energy you have and how you look. Get the balance right and you'll reap the benefits. But eat the wrong kinds of foods too often, skip meals on a regular basis, or overload your body with processed snacks, and your health will soon suffer.

The *Summer Detox* is designed to restore your energy levels, improve your health and make you look and feel a lot better. It's not about calorie counting, strict dieting or measuring out tiny portions of food. It doesn't even require self-discipline, denial or restraint. It's a healthy way of eating – based on ordinary foods – that fits in with your body's natural appetite and nutritional needs. You'll never feel hungry, you'll eat only the foods you like and you won't even need to spend much time cooking. In 14 days, you'll be bursting with health and vitality. Interested? Take the health and diet challenge to find out how healthy (or unhealthy) you are right now and whether you're ready to start the *Summer Detox*.

Health and Diet Challenge

HEALTH	DIET
I feel lacklustre and under the weather Yes/No	I often eat when I'm not hungry Yes/No
I often feel tired and lethargic Yes/No	I often skip breakfast Yes/No
I don't have much energy Yes/No	I often snack instead of eating proper meals Yes/No
I often find it difficult to get motivated Yes/No	I don't eat five portions of fresh fruit and vegetables daily Yes/No
I feel run down Yes/No	I often crave certain foods Yes/No
I often get the 'blues' Yes/No	Sometimes I can't stop eating Yes/No
I seem to get one cold or infection after another Yes/No	I eat the wrong foods when I'm bored, stressed or annoyed Yes/No
My last cold lingered for more than seven days Yes/No	If I see food, I have to eat it Yes/No
I am prone to skin problems, e.g. acne, dryness, eczema Yes/No	I have a sweet tooth Yes/No
I've noticed my hair falling out more than usual Yes/No	I drink soft drinks or fizzy drinks every day Yes/No
My hair is dull or very dry Yes/No	I eat sugary snacks (e.g. biscuits, chocolate, sweets, cakes) on most days Yes/No
My nails are very brittle or flaky Yes/No	
I get a headache at least once a week Yes/No	I eat salted snacks (e.g. crisps, tortillas) on most days Yes/No
I often feel bloated Yes/No	I drink alcohol on most days Yes/No
I often get constipated Yes/No	I can't get going without my morning fix of coffee or tea Yes/No
I often suffer from indigestion or heartburn Yes/No	I have takeaways at least once a week Yes/No
I often get diarrhoea or symptoms of irritable bowel syndrome (IBS) Yes/No	I eat ready-meals or ready-made sauces at least twice a week Yes/No
I get recurrent thrush (candida) Yes/No	I eat fast or fried food at least once a week Yes/No
I have cellulite Yes/No	I have dieted on and off for several years Yes/No
I suffer quite badly with premenstrual syndrome (PMS) each month Yes/No	I can't seem to lose weight Yes/No
	I put weight on very easily Yes/No

Your Answers

Health

If you answered 'yes' to ten or more statements in this section, you definitely need to improve your diet for the sake of your health. You would benefit from the *Summer Detox* right now! If you answered 'yes' to between five and ten statements, now is the time to take stock of your health and brush up on your eating habits before your symptoms get any worse. You will definitely notice a big improvement in your overall well-being by following the *Summer Detox*. Many health complaints, such as frequent colds, constipation, and lack of energy, are the result of poor eating habits, coupled with an inactive or stressful lifestyle. By paying closer attention to what you eat, you will start to eliminate these health symptoms, feel more energetic and look more radiant. Turn to the next chapter straight away!

Diet

If you answered 'yes' to ten or more statements in this section, you are almost certainly eating a poorly planned diet that isn't providing your body with the nutrients it needs to function properly. You are certainly ready for the *Summer Detox*! If you answered 'yes' to between five and ten statements, your diet is probably lacking in several important nutrients and you could be overloading your body with too much saturated fat, refined sugar and salt. Carry on like this and your health will soon suffer. The *Summer Detox* will not only improve your eating habits but will make you feel healthier. Eating erratically, skipping meals and snacking eventually take their toll on your energy levels and your health. Too much of any nutrient – whether it's sugar, fat, or alcohol – overburdens your digestive and elimination systems and increases the chances of fat storage. But dieting is not the answer. Instead, you need to make simple but lasting changes to the way you eat, choose nutritious foods, and learn to eat in a way that suits your lifestyle. The *Summer Detox* teaches you how to control your appetite naturally, eat only as much as your body needs and get all the nutrients you need for vibrant health. Read on!

energetic radiant

CHAPTER 4
TEN REASONS TO DETOX

Now you know your score on the health and diet challenge, you probably don't need much more convincing to start the *Summer Detox*. But it's good to know exactly what rewards you can expect in 14 days. Perhaps the prospect of wearing a swimsuit on the beach this summer will be all the motivation you need. Maybe you want to feel energetic and full of vigour over the coming summer months rather than lethargic and run down. Whatever you want out of the *Summer Detox*, here are ten good reasons to start it tomorrow:

1. YOU'LL LOSE EXCESS WEIGHT

Cut out the biscuits, takeaways and snacks, and eat instead plenty of whole grains, fruit, vegetables, beans, lentils and nuts, and you'll probably save a lot of unwanted calories. According to the world's largest study on successful weight loss, eating a diet high in fruit and vegetables is a vital part of losing weight and keeping it off. Fruit and vegetables are low in calories, virtually fat-free and filling. If you satisfy your appetite with fruit, vegetables, pulses and whole grains, you'll be less likely to turn to high-calorie snacks. But on this detox we don't want you to count calories and the chances are, once you've finished this eating plan, you'll never need to count calories again.

2. CELLULITE WILL DIMINISH

Lose fat and you lose cellulite – and that's great news for 85% of us women who are plagued by it. In fact, it affects 95% of women over 30! A healthy way of eating combined with exercise and skin care are the only proven ways to beat cellulite. So, follow the *Summer Detox* and you'll be well on the way to losing that unsightly cellulite.

WHAT IS CELLULITE?

Cellulite is simply fat. The reason it appears dimpled and puckered is that it lies very close to the skin's surface and is crisscrossed by weak collagen strands. This results in the typical bulging appearance of cellulite on your body. The reason women get it far more than men is the female hormone oestrogen, which favours fat storage on your thighs and bottom. So women tend to put weight on in these areas. Even exercise fanatics can have cellulite, although inactivity can also play a big role in its formation. Experts also believe that if you spend several hours a day sitting down, the lymphatic system slows down, which results in poor drainage from the fat cells.

3. YOU'LL HAVE MORE ENERGY

Vitality and health are the ultimate aims of the *Summer Detox*. By focusing on fruit, vegetables, salads, whole grains and pulses – foods that are fresh, have not been processed or overcooked and have not been adulterated with artificial additives – you'll be providing your body with all the nutrients it needs to work efficiently. You'll also be reducing the 'toxin' load on your system so you'll quickly begin to feel healthier and more energetic.

4. YOU'LL GET FEWER COLDS

On the *Summer Detox*, minor infections such as colds, sore throats and flu are less likely. Fruit and vegetables are the best ways to get high levels of vitamin C, betacarotene and other antioxidants in your diet, and research shows that people with high intakes of these nutrients have fewer sick days than others.

5. YOU'LL GET RID OF BLOATING

Swallowing too much air and eating in a rush are the most common causes of bloating. During the *Summer Detox* it is essential that you learn to take your time and sit down to eat. Chewing thoroughly and eating slowly will help reduce the amount of air swallowed with food. You should also avoid fizzy drinks as they introduce more unwanted air. Try plain water and still juices instead. Bloating is sometimes a reaction to certain foods. Cutting out or reducing common culprits such as yeast, wheat products, bran cereals or vegetables from the *Brassica* family (such as cabbage, Brussels sprouts, broccoli or cauliflower) may help.

6. YOU'LL ENJOY BETTER HEALTH

Numerous studies have linked a diet rich in fruit and vegetables with a lower risk of illness and diseases. According to the American Institute for Cancer Research, eating at least five servings of fruit and vegetables each day could prevent at least 20 per cent of cancer cases. Researchers from King's College, London found that people who eat at least two apples a week are up to 32 per cent less likely to develop asthma than people who eat fewer apples. And a University of Surrey study found that people who eat the most fruit and vegetables have stronger bones.

7. YOU CAN LOWER YOUR BLOOD PRESSURE

Eating more fruit and vegetables can lower blood pressure. This is due to the high content of potassium, which helps regulate the body's fluid balance. An Italian study found that 81 per cent of people with high blood pressure who started eating three to six servings of fruit and vegetables a day reduced their medication by half.

8. YOUR SKIN WILL LOOK SMOOTHER

Eating more fruit and vegetables – reducing the toxin load on your body – improves the clarity and texture of your skin. Your skin plays a vital role in ridding your body of unwanted substances and waste products (via sweating, skin oils and dead skin cells). According to an Australian study, people with diets high in fresh produce had smoother and less lined skin than those eating diets high in red meat and sugar.

9. YOUR HAIR WILL SHINE

The vitamins, minerals and phytonutrients in fruit and vegetables do wonders for your skin, hair and nails. A healthy diet tackles beauty problems from the inside; improving the rate of hair growth, cell renewal and collagen formation.

10. YOU'LL FEEL CALMER

Studies show that people whose diets are higher in fruit and vegetables find it easier to handle stress.

renewal

CHAPTER 5
WHAT YOUR BODY NEEDS

The *Summer Detox* has been designed to supply your body with all the nutrients it needs: protein, carbohydrates, healthy fats, vitamins, minerals, fibre and phytonutrients. Get the right balance and you'll have more energy and vitality to live life to the full.

The more varied your diet overall, the more likely you are to get all the nutrients you need. It may seem easier to stick to the same meals day after day but you could end up missing out on some nutrients. Eating lots of one or two kinds of food – even if it's fresh fruit or raw salad – doesn't make a balanced diet. You may be missing out on vital nutrients such as protein or calcium.

Here's the lowdown on your nutritional needs.

Carbohydrates for energy

Carbohydrates are your main source of energy. Your brain, nervous system and heart need a constant supply of carbohydrates. You also need them to fuel your daily activities.

Simple or complex?

There are two types of carbohydrates: simple (sugars) and complex (starches and fibre). Both are healthy. Simple carbohydrates occur naturally in fruit, vegetables, milk and honey. In this form, they come with a package of other nutrients (e.g. vitamins, minerals and fibre). But the processed form of sugars – in cakes, biscuits, confectionery and soft drinks – are regarded as 'empty calories'. Complex carbohydrates are found in grains and starchy vegetables such as potatoes and sweetcorn.

Go easy on fast carbs

Generally speaking, processed sugary or starchy foods (cakes, confectionery, white bread, sweetened breakfast cereals) – 'high glycaemic' foods – produce the fastest surge of glucose in your bloodstream. This energy buzz is usually only short-lived as your pancreas pumps out insulin to bring your blood sugar levels back down. Sometimes, it overcompensates and your blood sugar levels dip too low, resulting in fatigue and hunger. So you reach for your next sugar-fix. And the pattern repeats. Sounds familiar?

Go for the (slow) burn.

By contrast, most unprocessed carbohydrate foods (whole grains, fruit, beans and lentils) – 'low glycaemic' foods – release their energy slowly over a longer period. Combine them with protein or some healthy fat (for example, rice with beans, or fresh fruit with a handful of nuts) and you'll get a nice steady energy release. Which is precisely what you're aiming for.

FIBRE FACTS

Fibre helps your digestive system work properly and is alsouseful for weight control. There are two kinds of fibre; insoluble and soluble. Most plant foods contain both but the proportions vary. Good sources of insoluble fibre include whole grains (e.g. brown rice, rye bread, whole-wheat bread) and vegetables. These foods help speed the passage of food through your gut, prevent constipation and bowel problems and make you feel full after eating. Soluble fibre – found in oats, beans, lentils, fruit and vegetables – reduces blood cholesterol levels, helps control blood glucose levels by slowing glucose absorption, reduces hunger and improves appetite control.

Protein Power

Protein is made up of building blocks, which are used to repair cells, and to make enzymes, hormones and antibodies. Eight of these – the 'essential amino acids' – must be provided in your diet, while the remaining twelve can be made by your body. For your body to use food proteins properly, all eight essential amino acids have to be present. Animal proteins, as well as soya and Quorn, contain a good balance of the essential amino acids. But plant proteins (pulses, cereals, nuts and seeds) contain smaller amounts, so these need to be combined together (e.g. puy lentil and tomato salad with walnuts (see recipe on page 72); hummus (see recipe on page 103) with non-wheat bread) to make a full complement of amino acids. The general rule of thumb is to have grains and pulses, nuts and grains, or pulses and nuts together.

Healthy Fats

Very low-fat diets are a thing of the past. Not only are they bad for your health but also they won't necessarily make you lose weight! Scientists have discovered that a moderate intake of fat is better for you and is associated with better weight control long-term. That doesn't mean you can now feast on doughnuts and fry-ups! Rather, you should switch *saturated* (animal) fats and *processed* (hydrogenated) fats for *monounsaturated* fats and *essential* fats (omega-3 and omega-6 fats). And that's exactly what you'll be doing during the *Summer Detox*. Studies show that rebalancing your fat intake this way can lower your blood cholesterol, lower your blood pressure, boost your immunity – and even help you to lose weight!

healthy

Steer clear of saturated fats

Animal fats (meat, dairy products, butter) as well as products made with palm oil or palm kernel oil (a highly saturated fat) have no beneficial role in keeping the body healthy – they raise blood cholesterol levels and increase the risk of heart disease – so try to keep your intake as low as possible.

Ban processed fats

Processed or 'trans' fats, found in hydrogenated and partially hydrogenated oils, are even more harmful than saturated fats. They increase your levels of LDL (low density lipoprotein or 'bad') cholesterol while lowering levels of HDL (high density lipoprotein or 'good') cholesterol. A high LDL cholesterol level increases your heart disease risk; as does a low HDL cholesterol level (HDL protects against heart disease).

Monounsaturated fats are fine in moderation

Most of your fat intake should come from monounsaturated fats – olive oil, nuts, seeds, avocados and rapeseed oil. They help to lower harmful cholesterol levels and can cut your heart disease and cancer risk.

Go easy on polyunsaturated fats

In moderation, polyunsaturated fats – found in most vegetable oils and margarines - also reduce your heart disease risk, though less effectively than monounsaturated fats.

Boost omega-3 fats

You need only tiny amounts of omega-3 fats to keep you healthy but, as they are found in relatively few foods, many people struggle to meet the minimum requirement of 0.9g per day. For heart disease prevention, better oxygen delivery to your cells, reduced joint pain and stiffness and healthy skin, include one tablespoon of an omega-3-rich oil daily (see page 35) or a heaped tablespoon of nuts or seeds a day (see page 35).

Eat omega-6 fats in moderation

Omega-6 fats – found in sunflower oil, corn oil and most spreads and margarines – are also required for peak health. But most people currently eat too much omega-6 in relation to omega-3, which results in an imbalance of prostaglandins – 'mini' hormones – which are responsible for controlling blood clotting, inflammation and the immune system. By eating more omega-3s, you'll automatically improve the balance of these essential fats.

peak health

Saturated fats	Processed fats	Monounsaturated fats	Polyunsaturated fats	Omega-3 fats	Omega-6 fats
Cut down or avoid	Avoid	Eat instead	Eat in moderation	Eat more	Eat in moderation
Fatty meats	Foods listing hydrogenated fats or oils in the ingredients, such as:	Olive oil	Sunflower oil	Walnuts	Sunflower oil
Full-fat dairy products		Olive oil margarine	Corn oil	Walnut oil	Safflower oil
Butter		Rapeseed oil	Safflower oil	Pumpkin seeds	Sunflower oil margarine
Lard, shortening, dripping	Margarine	Avocados	Sunflower oil margarine	Pumpkinseed oil	Corn oil
Palm oil	Low-fat spread	Soya oil	Nuts and seeds	Flax seeds	Groundnut oil
Palm kernel oil	Pastries, pies and tarts	Peanuts, almonds, cashews		Flaxseed oil	Evening primrose oil
Margarine, spreads, biscuits, cakes, desserts, etc. made with palm or palm kernel oil	Biscuits	Peanut butter		Rapeseed oil	Sunflower and sesame seeds
Egg yolk	Cereal bars, breakfast bars	Mayonnaise		Soya oil	
	Cakes and bakery products			Sweet potatoes	
	Crackers			Omega-3 enriched eggs	
	Ice cream				
	Desserts and puddings				
	Fried food				

Vitamins and minerals

Vitamins support the immune system, help the brain function properly and help convert food into energy. They are important for healthy skin and hair, controlling growth and balancing hormones. Some vitamins – the B vitamins and vitamin C – must be provided by the diet each day, as they cannot be stored.

Minerals are needed for structural and regulatory functions, including bone strength, haemoglobin manufacture, fluid balance and muscle contraction (see the 'essential vitamin and mineral guide', pages 25–26).

Antioxidants

Antioxidants – which neutralise the effects of free radicals – include vitamins (betacarotene, vitamin C, vitamin E), minerals (such as selenium and zinc), and plant compounds called phytochemicals. You'll find them in fruit and vegetables, seeds, nuts, oils, whole grains, beans and lentils – foods that are at the heart of the *Summer Detox*! Many studies have indicated that a diet rich in these antioxidant foods protects against heart disease and cancer, delays ageing and prevents cataracts.

Here are the best food sources of antioxidants:

Vitamin C	Citrus fruit, berries, peppers
Vitamin E	Sunflower and nut oils, avocado, almonds, salmon*
Selenium	Brazil nuts, meat*, whole grains
Betacarotene	Carrots, apricots, red peppers, mango
Flavanoids	Fruit, vegetables, tea, garlic, red wine*
Lycopene	Tomatoes, watermelon

*Not included in the *Summer Detox*

Phytonutrients

Phytonutrients are compounds found naturally in fruit, vegetables, whole grains, beans, lentils, and soya products – again, foods that are at the heart of the *Summer Detox*. They include bioflavanoids, polyphenols, carotenoids, coumestrol, salicylates, sulphoramine, anthocyanins, flavanols, limonene, isoflavones and lutein (see Chapter 16 – Super Foods).

Most act as powerful antioxidants that work with vitamins and minerals to protect the body from degenerative diseases (such as heart disease and cancer), boost immunity and fight harmful bacteria and viruses. There are hundreds of different types of phytochemicals and the best way to make sure you get enough of them is to eat at least five daily portions of fruits and vegetables. Aim to eat a variety of different colours (see page 32). Remember, the more intense the colour, the higher the phytonutrient level will be.

antioxidants

Essential vitamin and mineral guide

Vitamin	Needed for	Best food sources*
A	Vision in dim light; healthy skin and linings of the digestive tract, nose and throat.	Full fat dairy products; meat; offal; oily fish; margarine.
Beta-carotene	Antioxidant which protects against certain cancers; converts into vitamin A.	Fruit and vegetables e.g. apricots, peppers, tomatoes, mangoes, broccoli, squash, carrots, watercress.
Thiamin	Releasing energy from carbohydrates; healthy nerves and digestive system.	Wholemeal bread and cereals; pulses; meat; sunflower seeds.
Riboflavin	Releasing energy from carbohydrates; healthy skin, eyes and nerves.	Milk and dairy products; meat; eggs, soya products.
Niacin	Releasing energy from carbohydrates; healthy skin, nerves and digestion.	Meat and offal; nuts; milk and dairy products; eggs; wholegrain cereals.
Vitamin B6 (pyridoxine)	Metabolism of protein, carbohydrate, fat; red blood cell manufacture; healthy immune system.	Pulses; nuts; eggs; cereals; fish; bananas.
Folic Acid	Formation of DNA and red blood cells; reduces risk of spina bifida in developing babies in the womb.	Green leafy vegetables; yeast extract; pulses; nuts; pulses; citrus fruit.
Vitamin B12	Formation of red blood cells; energy metabolism.	Milk and dairy products; meat; fish; fortified breakfast cereals, soya products and yeast extract.
Vitamin C	Healthy connective tissue, bones, teeth, blood vessels, gums and teeth; promotes immune function; helps iron absorption.	Fruit and vegetables (e.g. raspberries, blackcurrants, kiwi, oranges, peppers, broccoli, cabbage, tomatoes).
Vitamin D	Building strong bones; absorption of calcium and phosphorus.	Sunlight; oily fish; fortified margarine and breakfast cereals, eggs.
Vitamin E	Antioxidant that helps protect against heart disease; promotes normal cell growth and development.	Vegetable oils; oily fish; nuts; seeds; egg yolk; avocado.

*Not all these foods are included in the *Summer Detox*

Mineral	Needed for	Best food sources*
Calcium	Building bone and teeth; blood clotting; nerve and muscle function.	Milk and dairy products; sardines; dark green leafy vegetables; pulses; brazil nuts, almonds, figs, and sesame seeds
Iron	Formation of red blood cells; oxygen transport; prevents anaemia.	Meat and offal; wholegrain cereals; fortified breakfast cereals; pulses; green leafy vegetables, nuts, sesame and pumpkin seeds.
Zinc	Healthy immune system; wound healing; healthy skin; growth.	Eggs; wholegrain cereals; meat; nuts and seeds.
Magnesium	Healthy bones; muscle and nerve function; cell formation.	Cereals; fruit; vegetables; milk, nuts and seeds.
Potassium	Fluid balance; muscle and nerve function.	Fruit; vegetables; cereals, nuts and seeds.
Sodium**	Fluid balance; muscle and nerve function.	Salt; processed meat, ready meals, sauces, soup, cheese, bread.
Selenium	Antioxidant that helps protect against heart disease and cancer.	Cereals; vegetables; dairy products; meat; eggs, nuts and seeds.

*Not all these foods are included in the *Summer Detox*

** Too much sodium (salt) can raise blood pressure. On average we eat about 9g of salt daily. The government advise a maximum of 2.5g sodium (6.5g salt) daily for men and 2g sodium (5g salt) daily for women (1g of sodium is equivalent to 2.5g of salt).

balance
health

CHAPTER 6
SIX RULES FOR SUCCESS

The main focus of the *Summer Detox* is nutrient-packed fresh food. Over the next 14 days, you will leave behind processed foods that are full of sugar, fat, artificial additives and salt, and eat instead lots of natural unprocessed foods: fresh fruit, vegetables, salads, whole grains, beans, lentils, nuts, seeds and healthy oils.

This means that you will be getting lots more vitamins, minerals, antioxidants and fibre. These nutrients are vital for keeping your body in peak health, allowing your digestive system to process foods efficiently and your elimination system to carry waste products out of the body. They also support the immune system, increasing your resistance to colds and minor infections.

Eating foods close to their natural state allows your body to rebalance and function more efficiently. During the *Summer Detox*, you'll learn to listen to your body and eat only what you really need. You won't go hungry; instead you'll feel satisfied and relaxed about eating. You'll lose unwanted weight as your body adjusts your appetite to your needs.

Here are the six golden rules to help you succeed on the *Summer Detox*:

1. EAT FRESH FOOD

Eating fresh food means choosing foods that are rich in vital nutrients. As far as possible, try to buy fruit and vegetables that have been grown locally (not imported), that are in season and are not damaged or discoloured in any way. You may need to shop more than once a week as many fresh foods don't keep for more than a few days.

Food starts to lose its vitamins once it is exposed to air and light so store vegetables and soft fruits in a cool, dark place. Cut and prepare fruit and vegetables just before using them (see also page 32).

2. EAT RAW OR LIGHTLY COOKED FOOD

Uncooked fruit and vegetables contains the most vitamins. Once food is cooked, the vitamin content is reduced so try to eat mostly raw or lightly cooked foods during the *Summer Detox*. That way, you'll be getting the maximum amount of vital nutrients. Raw fruit and vegetables feature in many of the tasty recipes that follow, such as salads, soups, smoothies and juices. Of course, certain foods (potatoes and dried beans and lentils, for example) need to be cooked to break down the cell walls, soften the starch and make them digestible.

When you cook vegetables, try steaming them over a little boiling water so that they retain most of their vitamins. If you must boil your vegetables, use only a little water (about 1–2cm) and add them to the pan only once the water has come to the boil. Cook them until they are only just tender, not soft and soggy. Some vegetables, such as mangetout, green beans or broccoli, taste better when they are still slightly crunchy. Stir-frying is also a good cooking method as the food is cooked in a little oil at a high temperature for a brief time, so the vitamins are kept sealed in.

3. CUT THE JUNK!

During the *Summer Detox* you should aim to cut out heavily processed foods from your diet. Foods such as biscuits, crisps and salty snacks, ready-made puddings and desserts, sweets, fizzy drinks and chocolate bars are practically devoid of vitamins, minerals and fibre. They are also packed with saturated fat, sugar, salt and artificial additives. By cutting the junk, you are reducing any toxic burden on your body.

Eating 'whole' and 'natural' foods provides valuable fibre that helps your digestive system work efficiently. You'll also get more vitamins, minerals and phytonutrients, plant substances that protect against illness and improve your all-round health.

4. DRINK WATER

Make a habit of drinking regularly. No, not the alcoholic kind, but water and juices instead. Have a glass of water first thing in the morning and have frequent drink breaks during your day. Aim for 6–8 glasses (1–1½ litres) daily, more in hot weather or when you exercise. It's better to drink little and often rather than swigging large amounts in one go, which promotes urination and a greater loss of fluid.

Carry a bottle of water with you everywhere. To the office, in the car, out shopping. It'll be a constant reminder to drink. It need not be expensive bottled water. A simple water bottle will do – just refill with tap water.

Watching your urine is the best way to check your body's hydration. Dark gold-coloured urine is a sure sign that you're low on fluid. Drink plenty of water and aim for light yellow-coloured urine.

5. EAT WHEN YOU ARE HUNGRY AND ENJOY IT

The *Summer Detox* is not a starvation diet! While you are following the eating plan you should never be hungry, because you will be eating filling nutritious food. If you feel peckish between meals, don't deny your hunger or deprive yourself. Instead, have a healthy snack (see page 39) and don't feel guilty about it.

During the next 14 days, learn to listen to your body's hunger signals. This may take a bit of practice to begin with. It can be difficult at first to work out whether it's food or drink that your body really needs or whether you just think you're hungry due to boredom, stress or habit. If you have no idea when you are hungry, don't eat, as it means you aren't hungry. On the other hand, don't wait until you are very hungry or starving before eating. Otherwise you will end up eating the wrong foods or overeating.

Try to gauge how much food your body really needs. Unlike other diets, the *Summer Detox* does not give precise quantities of foods to eat. Sometimes your body may want a lot of food, sometimes it wants just a little. Respond to your body's needs and simply eat the amount that is right for you. Over the next 14 days you will become attuned to your body's needs and learn to eat the types and amounts of food that are right for you.

Eating should be a pleasurable experience, so make time to shop for, prepare and savour your food. The *Summer Detox* provides you with 14 suggested menus and 80 tasty recipes, but you can interchange daily menus or substitute different recipes if you prefer (see page 38 – at the start of Chapter 8).

Within the menu choices, select foods you like, foods that suit you and foods that satisfy you. Do that and you'll find it easy to stick to the eating plan for 14 days … and beyond. On the other hand, force yourself to eat foods that don't suit you and you'll certainly slip back to old eating habits after a few days.

When you sit down to eat, taste every mouthful and enjoy every bite. Stop eating the moment you stop savouring the food or the moment you are full. It's easier to notice you are full if you pay attention while you are eating. That way, your body sends you a message that it is satisfied. But if you don't concentrate while you eat, you may miss your body telling you it's full, leading you to override the feeling of fullness and overeat.

Another reason many people find it hard to listen to their appetite is because they eat the wrong foods. Processed foods such as biscuits, cakes, chocolate and crisps are high in calories but lacking in fibre, water and vital nutrients. They don't fill you up readily nor satisfy your appetite. So your hunger signals become confused and you overeat. Eliminate these foods and eat instead lots of fibre-rich nutrient-packed foods – fruit, vegetables, whole grains and pulses – and your appetite will quickly readjust.

6. MAKE YOUR SKIN GLOW

Your skin is alive. It's the largest organ of your body and helps to get rid of toxins by excreting about 1/2kg (1lb) of waste every day. That's why it's essential to keep it in top condition. During a long winter we tend to neglect our skin (other than that on the face) and so by summer time, when we're thinking about baring our bodies on the beach, it's often looking rather grey and unhealthy. But the wonderful thing is that skin can be made to glow very easily. I've put together a little plan and if you follow it, the quality of your skin will improve dramatically.

Dry skin brushing

I've found that this is the most beneficial and cheapest way to alter the skin on your body. Buy a dry brittle body brush (I prefer this to a loofah). Once or twice a day, brush your whole body vigorously starting with the underneath of your feet, your legs, bum and tum, always brushing upwards towards your heart. Then continue with the palms of your hands, your arms, shoulders, back and chest (although be more gentle here as the skin can be sensitive). You'll find that once you've done this your skin feels very warm and the circulation of blood near the surface has increased — which is why it's a great way to help beat cellulite.

Oil or body cream

Next have your shower, bath or steam and either while you're in the bath or afterwards when you're dry, try a bit of massage on the thighs, bum and tum. Use simple techniques such as pushing your fingertips into your flesh or pushing your hands in opposite directions so that they twist the flesh. Don't be too gentle either — you want to start to physically break down the fatty deposits just below the skin surface and boost your circulation. Once you're dry, work some anti-cellulite oil or cream into your thighs, bum and tum. For the rest of your body use whichever cream you favour. Remember to use plenty of cream on your chest and bust as this part of the skin can age quite rapidly, so you need to keep it well moisturised. I've found that using the cream I use on my face (Helena Rubenstein Collagenist) on my chest too can change how it looks in a matter of days. Try it. It works.

Getting ready for the sun

Once you've brushed and soaked yourself in cream for a couple of weeks, I promise that your skin will be ready for baring on the beach. Treat yourself to a bit of false tan beforehand and you'll feel a whole lot better. Mind you, if you have been sunbathing, don't be too harsh with the dry skin brushing as it will take all of your tan off with it. If you want to leave the dry skin brushing until you're home again, do so. But keep your skin moisturised and continue with the self massage.

glowing skin

CHAPTER 7
WHAT TO EAT

The *Summer Detox* is not a starvation regime and it's not about counting calories. It's all about eating more and enjoying tasty meals! That's right. During the next 14 days, you will be eating more of the delicious healthy foods that do your body good, boost your energy levels, make your skin glow and help you lose inches.

Fruit and vegetables

3+ portions of vegetables a day
2+ portions of fruit a day

Fruit and vegetables are central to the *Summer Detox* eating plan. They are full of antioxidant vitamins, minerals, fibre and phytonutrients (see page 24), which are vital for peak health. A high level of fruit and vegetables in your diet helps to boost your immunity and protect your body from cancer, heart disease and bowel disease. Eat fresh foods in season when they are less expensive and at their best.

The vitamin content of fruit and vegetables is reduced by heat, so try to eat some raw food every day. As it is not always convenient or practical to eat raw food, here are some tips to help minimise vitamin and mineral losses when cooking fruit and vegetables:

- Wash and prepare vegetables just before cooking them. Once they are cut, they start to lose vitamins. Put them straight into boiling water or steam them.
- Cook vegetables as lightly as possible; they should be firm and tender, not soft and soggy.

- Do not reheat leftover cooked vegetables.
- If fresh vegetables are not available, use frozen food. It has a similar nutritional content.
- Stir-frying is a good alternative to steaming or boiling as it preserves most of the nutrients and flavour.

EAT YOUR GREENS . . . AND REDS, PURPLES, YELLOWS AND ORANGES

It's a good idea to eat something yellow, red, orange, purple, green and white every day. Each colour relates to different phytonutrients in the food, with each having a different health benefit. Orange, yellow and red foods (e.g. carrots, apricots, mangoes) get their colour from betacarotene and other carotenoids; tomatoes and watermelon are rich in lycopene (another carotenoid). These carotenoids are powerful antioxidants and help keep you young-looking and healthy. Green foods (broccoli, peas, spinach, etc.) are rich in magnesium, iron and chlorophyll (a terrific antioxidant and natural detoxifier); red and purple foods like grapes, blackberries and strawberries get their colour from anthocyanins, which are even more powerful than vitamin C at fighting harmful free radicals, and white foods (e.g. apples, pears, cauliflower) contain flavanols, which protect against heart disease and cancer. Also, the more intense the colour, the more phytonutrients you'll be getting.

WHAT'S A PORTION OF FRUIT?

About the size of a tennis ball, for instance:
- 1 medium fruit, e.g. apple, orange, banana, peach
- 2 small fruit, e.g. kiwi fruit, plums, satsumas, apricots
- 1 cupful of berries, e.g. strawberries, raspberries, cherries, grapes
- 1 large slice of large fruit, e.g. melon, mango, pineapple

WHAT'S A PORTION OF VEGETABLES?

About the size of your hand, for instance:
- 1 dessert bowl of salad vegetables, e.g. lettuce, salad leaves
- 2 tablespoons of cooked vegetables, e.g. broccoli, cauliflower, carrots, green beans, peppers, peas, mangetout

EAT 5

Only 1 in 10 people eat enough fruit and vegetables to protect themselves from cancer and heart disease. The World Health Organisation has estimated that five servings of fruit and vegetables provide us with at least the minimum doses of vitamins, minerals and fibre we need to stay healthy. Experts at the US National Cancer Institute believe that nine servings a day may be even better. Their mantra, 'Eating 5 to 9 and Feeling Fine: Fruits and Vegetables Anytime', is supported by studies showing that people who chewed down their greens – and reds and yellows – had half the risk of certain cancers than those who didn't reach the recommended range. According to the American Dietetic Association you should try to have two to three servings of fruit and then really try to bulk up on the vegetables because they are so low in calories.

Grains, bread and pasta

Grains are the main sources of complex carbohydrates in the *Summer Detox*. These foods provide energy for daily activities and exercise. They are also rich in fibre, B vitamins (such as thiamin and niacin), vitamin E and minerals (such as iron). Choose the wholegrain (unrefined) varieties rather than refined 'white' versions, which have been stripped of most of their vitamins, minerals and fibre.

The *Summer Detox* excludes wheat and encourages you to try other grains for 14 days. If you have previously eaten a lot of wheat products – pasta, cereals and bread – you may have developed a mild sensitivity to these foods and become prone to symptoms such as bloating and wind. Swapping wheat for other grains – oats, brown rice, millet, quinoa – or for sweet potatoes or potatoes, may help to alleviate your symptoms. After the 14-day *Summer Detox*, you can try gradually reintroducing wheat products in your diet.

Here is a guide to the grains featured in the *Summer Detox*:

Rice

Wholegrain (brown) rice is far more nutritious than the white variety, which is almost devoid of vitamins, minerals and fibre. Wholegrain rice includes the outer bran layers of the grain, which contain the fibre, magnesium, phosphorus, thiamin (vitamin B1) and iron that are necessary in our diet. It makes a delicious base for summer salads (see recipe on page 75) or fillings for summer vegetables such as roasted peppers with millet and cashew nuts (see recipe on page 83). To save time, try the parboiled variety, which takes only ten minutes to cook.

Oats

Oats contain soluble fibre, which makes them a super source of slow-release energy. Eaten regularly, they help to lower blood cholesterol levels and control blood pressure. Oats are also a good source of B vitamins, iron, magnesium and zinc. The easiest way to include oats in your diet is by eating porridge, muesli (see recipes on pages 57–59) or fruit crumbles (see recipe on page 113).

Millet

Millet is a small round grain, a staple from Africa, China and India, and a good source of magnesium and iron. It can be boiled and used as an alternative to rice. You can also buy millet flakes and use them in muesli, porridge or fruit crumbles.

Rye

Rye is the main ingredient in rye bread and rye crackers. Unlike wheat, rye contains no gluten so switching breads may reduce symptoms like bloating and wind if you are sensitive to gluten. It is rich in vitamin E, iron and zinc.

Quinoa

Quinoa (pronounced 'keenwa') contains more protein than any grain. Technically, it is a fruit, not a grain but, as it is used as an alternative to rice or pasta (see summer vegetables with quinoa on page 92), it is included in this section. It is rich in iron, magnesium and vitamin E. Quinoa is also low in fat and most of its oil is unsaturated, providing the essential fatty acids.

DO YOU HAVE A FOOD ALLERGY?

One in three people believe they are allergic to at least one kind of food but, according to a British study, only one in fifty actually are. Most doctors reserve the term allergy for life-threatening reactions, such as the one some people have to peanuts. Here, the body produces antibodies (IgE), which trigger the allergic response. If you suspect that you have a food allergy, you should see your doctor who can refer you to a hospital or allergy clinic for a skin-prick test and blood test.

With food intolerances or sensitivities – such as gluten or wheat – the body doesn't produce antibodies against the offending food and the symptoms may be vague – fatigue, headaches, bloating, loose bowel movements, for example. Eliminating or cutting down on the offending food for a few weeks often leads to an improvement in symptoms. However, a true wheat allergy, as in coeliac disease – a lifelong intolerance to gluten, which affects the lining of the bowel – should be diagnosed by a doctor and requires individual advice from a dietitian before starting on a gluten-free diet.

Beans, lentils and peas

Beans, lentils and peas (also known as pulses) are packed with protein, complex carbohydrates, fibre, B vitamins, iron, zinc, manganese and magnesium so they provide a healthy alternative to animal proteins. They also provide soluble fibre, which combines with water in the gut to make a gummy substance that slows digestion and absorption of food. This helps regulate blood glucose levels and makes you feel full for longer. They also help to lower blood cholesterol and prevent heart disease. Chickpeas are particularly valuable because they contain fructo-oligosaccharides, a type of fibre that increases the friendly bacteria of the gut – especially useful if your gut bacteria get upset by travel or stress.

Here are some ways to make the most of beans, lentils and peas:

- If cooking dried pulses, soak them overnight, drain and cook them in fresh water until they are soft (follow the instructions on the packet). Add a little salt-free vegetable bouillon, if you wish, but do not add salt until they have been cooked.
- For convenience, buy tinned pulses. Drain and rinse if they have been tinned in salted water.
- Help your digestive system adapt to pulses by starting off with only small quantities (1–2 tablespoons twice a week), and gradually increasing the amount (up to 3–4 tablespoons daily) as you get accustomed to them.
- Red kidney beans, chickpeas and flageolet beans are delicious in salads (see recipes), adding texture as well as vital nutrients.

Healthy oils

Another way to get essential fats is to use cold-pressed oils. Rapeseed oil, extra virgin olive oil, linseed (flaxseed) oil, walnut oil and sesame oil are rich in the omega-3 and omega-6 fatty acids, which protect against heart disease. Here are some tips on using oils:

- If oils are your only source of essential fats you need about one level tablespoon a day.
- Use omega-3-rich cold-pressed oils (such as walnut oil and linseed (flaxseed) oil) in dressings or stir a spoonful into soups and sauces. Don't fry with these oils as their nutritional value will be reduced by high temperatures.
- When buying olive oil, choose extra virgin olive oil as it is cold-pressed and contains higher levels of antioxidants than ordinary olive oil. It is rich in monounsaturated oil and omega-6 oils and can be used for stir-frying as well as dressings.
- Try cold-pressed oil blends, containing a mixture of linseed (flaxseed) oil and other oils to give you a good balance of omega-3 and omega-6. Store them in the fridge to stop them from going rancid.

Nuts and seeds

Far from being 'fattening', nuts and seeds are nutritional powerhouses. They are full of essential fats, protein, fibre, B vitamins, iron, zinc and magnesium. Although they provide a lot of calories per 100g, they come mainly from heart-healthy monounsaturated oils – which help to lower blood cholesterol levels and protect against heart attacks – and the vital omega-3 and omega-6 oils (see below). According to a US study of 21,000 male doctors, those who ate two one-ounce servings of nuts each week were 30 per cent less likely to die from heart disease than those who rarely or never ate nuts. Here are some ways of reaping the benefits of nuts and seeds:

- To achieve the optimal intake of essential fats, you need to eat around a heaped tablespoon of nuts or seeds a day. Eat as snacks, sprinkled on salads or breakfast cereals or included in the recipes.
- Buy the unsalted kind without spicy or sugary coatings. Toasting them lightly under a hot grill or in a hot oven for a few minutes brings out their flavour.
- Pumpkin seeds and linseeds (flaxseeds) are particularly rich in the omega-3 oils, which are lacking in most people's diets. Linseeds have a very tough outer husk, which is practically impenetrable by digestive enzymes, so you'll need to grind them in a coffee grinder to benefit from the oils. Add to muesli, yoghurt, shakes and smoothies.
- When buying nuts and seeds, check the use-by date is several months away to ensure they are as fresh as possible. Store in an airtight container in a dark place as they can quickly turn rancid if exposed to light and air.

Non-dairy produce

You should avoid cow's milk products – milk, cheese, butter, cream and yoghurt – during the *Summer Detox*. Many people find that symptoms such as bloating, wind, nasal congestion or a runny nose improve once they give their system a break from dairy products. (However, you may gradually reintroduce these foods after 14 days.) Instead, use non-dairy equivalents of milk such as rice milk, soya milk, almond milk and oat milk. Soya and almond milk provide protein and most brands are fortified with calcium. Non-dairy milks usually contain healthy oils (e.g. rapeseed), which boosts their content of healthy unsaturated fats.

Soya 'yoghurt' may also be substituted for dairy yoghurt, but avoid the highly sweetened varieties. Try the plain variety or make your own (see recipe on page 60) then stir in puréed fruit, pure fruit spread or honey.

Tofu is bean curd made from soya beans. You can buy it from supermarkets and it is a useful way of getting protein and calcium while you are following the *Summer Detox*. It doesn't have much taste on its own but readily absorbs the flavours of any marinade or dressing (see the recipe for tofu mayonnaise on page 98, for example). Try it with stir-fries, threaded onto vegetable kebabs (see recipe for vegetable kebabs on page 89) or in smoothies and shakes (see recipes for power punch on page 139 and banana tofu shake on page 137) .

Herbs and spices

Avoid adding salt to food and keep salt in cooking to a minimum on the *Summer Detox*. If you must use salt or where it is suggested in a recipe, use sea salt (it has a more intense taste so you use less), herb salt (available from health stores) or a low-sodium salt (available from supermarkets).

You can enhance the flavour of your food with herbs, such as basil, oregano, mint and parsley, lemon juice, lime juice, freshly ground black peppers, chilli, cider and balsamic vinegar. Many of the recipes in Chapters 10 and 11 include fresh herbs, which are rich in iron and vitamin C, but you can substitute the dried variety if necessary. Spices, such as coriander and ginger, are also good for detoxing as they help digestion.

Food to avoid

During the *Summer Detox*, you should avoid:
- Ready meals
- Ready-bought sauces and salad dressings
- Foods containing artificial additives
- 'Low-calorie' foods or 'diet' drinks
- Salty snack foods, e.g. crisps
- Sugar and sugary foods, e.g. biscuits, cakes, chocolate bars, sweets
- Salty foods
- Meat and fish
- Dairy products
- Eggs
- Alcoholic drinks
- Coffee, tea and other caffeine-containing drinks
- Ordinary (wheat) bread, pasta and flour

CUTTING DOWN ON CAFFEINE

If you normally drink more than three cups of coffee, tea or cola a day, you must cut back gradually before you begin the *Summer Detox*. Do not try to give up caffeine from one day to the next, otherwise you may get withdrawal symptoms such as persistent headaches and irritability. Many people report greater energy levels and a better sense of wellbeing once they wean themselves off caffeine.

Shopping list

Use the following shopping list as a basis for developing your own list. It includes most of the foods you'll be eating over the next 14 days so gives you a good idea of the types of products to look out for in the shops. Add or take off foods according to the menus you select and your own food preferences.

Drinks
Mineral water
Herbal or fruit teas
Rooibosch tea
Green tea
Pure fruit juice
Vegetable juice

Fruit
Apples
Apricots
Avocado
Bananas
Blackberries
Blueberries
Cherries
Clementines
Dates
Dried apricots
Figs
Grapefruit
Kiwi fruits
Lemons
Limes
Mango
Melon
Olives
Papaya
Peaches
Pears

Pineapple
Plums
Raspberries
Raisins
Rhubarb
Satsumas
Strawberries
Sultanas
Tomatoes
Watermelon

Vegetables
Asparagus
Baby corn
Broccoli
Cabbage
Cauliflower
Celery
Courgettes
Cucumber
Fennel
Garlic
Green beans
Lamb's lettuce
Lettuce
Mangetout
Mixed salad leaves
Mushrooms
Onions
Peas (fresh or frozen)

Peppers – red, yellow,
orange or green
Potatoes
Pumpkin
Rocket
Spinach
Squash
Spring onions
Sugar-snap peas
Sweet potatoes
Watercress

Grains
Millet (whole grain)
Millet flakes
Non-wheat pasta
(e.g. corn, rice, millet)
Oats
Rice flour
Quinoa
Whole grain (brown) and
arborio (risotto) rice
Breads and crispbreads
Oatcakes
Pumpernickel bread
Rice cakes
Rye bread
Rye crackers
Wheat-free bread

Beans and lentils
(select either tinned or
dried versions)
Black-eyed beans
Butter beans
Chick peas
Flageolet beans
Hummus
Lentils (red, green, brown)
Red kidney beans
Sprouted beans (e.g. mung, alfalfa)

Nuts and seeds
Select unsalted whole, flaked
or ground nuts, such as:
Almonds
Brazils
Cashews
Hazelnuts
Linseeds (flaxseeds)
Peanuts
Pecans
Pine nuts
Pumpkinseeds
Sesame seeds
Sunflower seeds
Walnuts

Cold-pressed oils
Cold-pressed oil blends containing
a mixture of omega-3 rich oils

Extra-virgin olive oil
Linseed (flaxseed)
Pumpkinseed
Rapeseed
Sesame
Sweet almond oil
Sunflower
Walnut

Non-dairy foods
Almond milk
Coconut milk
Oat milk
Rice milk
Soya milk
Soya yoghurt
Tofu

Other
Selection of fresh and dried herbs
(e.g. basil, parsley, mint, coriander)
Spices (e.g. cinnamon, ground
cumin or coriander)
Chillis
Dijon or whole grain mustard
Fresh ginger
Light soy sauce
Honey
Cider, red wine or balsamic vinegar
Dairy-free spread

CHAPTER 8
14-DAY DETOX MENU PLAN

Choose the right time for it

You should pick a fortnight when you will have few commitments or distractions so that you can keep focused on your eating plan. Otherwise, you may find that if you take on too many new challenges and become overstressed, you're more likely to give up . We all know how easy it is to reach for chocolate or a glass of wine when we're tired, stressed or angry! Don't do it.

Go for 7 or 14

Ideally, you should follow the menu plan for 14 days. If you can only manage 7 days, you'll still benefit but if you can continue for longer then you will notice a bigger improvement in your energy levels, skin complexion and body shape. Although weight loss is not the major objective of this plan, you may find that you shed pounds. By filling up on fibre-packed nutritious foods instead, you can expect to lose weight. And the longer you stick to the detox plan, the more weight you'll lose!

Be flexible

Use this 14-day menu plan as a base for developing your own eating plan. While the daily menus have been carefully balanced to provide the right proportions of nutrients to keep you healthy, it is possible to swap meals between different days. For example, you may prefer to have the lunch suggested for Day 7 on Day 1 instead. Or you may fancy having the evening meal suggestion for Day 10 on Day 3.

Eat in tune with your body

The lunches and evening meals are also interchangeable. So, if you prefer to have your main meal at lunchtime, you may wish to have the suggested evening meal at midday and the suggested lunch in the evening.

Change a few ingredients

Most of the recipes can be adapted slightly according to which ingredients you have to hand. You don't have to stick rigidly to the stated ingredients. For example, with the recipe for Vegetable Kebabs you may use other summer vegetables (sweetcorn or fennel) instead of the courgettes or peppers.

Keep favourite recipes

Feel free to adapt your favourite recipes to fit in with the detox principles. By omitting or substituting a few ingredients in your own recipe, you can incorporate it into the *Summer Detox* plan. This is useful when you have to cook for your family or friends. Alternatively, take out your portion before adding, say, the cheese or meat to the remainder of the dish for everyone else. Easy!

Keep changing

Whether you decide to use all of the recipes in this eating plan or you include some of your own, remember to vary the foods you eat daily. The more varied your diet overall, the more likely you are to get all the vitamins, minerals and phytonutrients you need. It may seem easier to begin with to stick to the same meals day after day, but you could end up missing out on some nutrients.

Listen to your body

You'll notice that this eating plan does not state precise amounts of some of the foods, for example, accompanying rice or fresh fruit. That's because we all have different energy and nutritional needs and, therefore, should eat different quantities of food (see page 29 – Rule 5 in '6 rules for success'). It may sound obvious but one of the biggest failings of most weight-loss diets is that they assume one size fits all and prescribe the same diet for everyone. That's madness! So, how do you know how much to eat? Listen to your body and respond to your appetite. Eat when you are hungry, eat only as much as your body needs – and no more – and then stop eating when you are satisfied. Believe me, this really works – provided you are choosing naturally filling nutrient-packed foods (like vegetables, fruit and whole grains) and not high-calorie sugary foods.

Get ahead

To make life easier, you may wish to prepare some of the dishes in advance or cook larger amounts so that you have a meal ready – in the fridge or freezer - when you are pressed for time. Try to prepare vegetables, salads and fruit salads just before you eat them, though, as they start to lose their vitamins through oxidation once they are cut.

Get a drinking habit

Remember to drink plenty of water, herb or fruit tea. Aim for 6–8 glasses or cups daily, more when it's hot or when you exercise. This helps the detoxification process and keeps your system healthy.

Dine with friends

Can you entertain and eat with friends on the *Summer Detox* plan? Definitely! Eating is a social thing so we've supplied recipes that not only taste delicious but are good enough to share with friends. Three menus for summer entertaining are given at the end of this chapter on pages 54–55.

Snacks

If you feel hungry between meals, have a healthy snack. Remember, this diet is not about starvation, hunger or denial so you must never feel guilty about eating. Here are some suggestions on what to eat:

- A bowl of strawberries, raspberries, blueberries or blackberries
- A bunch of grapes
- A peach, nectarine or kiwi fruit
- A couple of plums or apricots
- A large slice of melon or pineapple
- A bowl of fresh fruit salad
- A banana
- Vegetable crudités with hummus or avocado dip
- A small handful of unsalted nuts (plain or toasted)
- A small handful of (unsulphured) dried fruit
- A small handful of seeds (plain or toasted)
- A glass of juice (see recipes on pages 121–8)
- A smoothie (see recipes on pages 130–9)

day 1

BREAKFAST

Summer fruit muesli (see recipe on page 57)

LUNCH

Slice of rye (or non-wheat) bread

Hummus (see recipe on page 103)

Crudités, e.g. carrot, cucumber, red pepper, cherry tomatoes, celery

Fresh fruit

EVENING MEAL

Stir-fried summer vegetables (see recipe on page 94)

Wholegrain (brown) rice mixed with toasted cashew nuts

day 2

BREAKFAST

Raisin and cinnamon oat porridge (see recipe on page 59)

LUNCH

Carrot and almond salad (see recipe on page 69)

Plain soya yoghurt with fresh fruit

EVENING MEAL

Summer vegetables with quinoa (see recipe on page 92)

Papaya, mango and lime salad (see recipe on page 110)

day 3

BREAKFAST

Plain soya yoghurt (shop-bought or see recipe on page 60)

Bowl of fresh fruit e.g. nectarines, plums

LUNCH

Lamb's lettuce salad with walnuts (see recipe page 65)

Rye crispbread

EVENING MEAL

Baked sweet potato, drizzle of extra virgin olive oil or walnut oil

Ratatouille (see recipe on page 88)

Bowl of fresh summer fruit, e.g. strawberries or raspberries,
with tofu 'cream' (see recipe on page 118) (if liked)

day 4

BREAKFAST

Raspberry and soya shake (see recipe on page 138)

LUNCH

Summer vegetable soup (see recipe on page 93)

Slice of rye (or non-wheat) bread

EVENING MEAL

Puy lentil and tomato salad with walnuts (see recipe on page 72)

Half a cantaloupe or galia melon cut into cubes

day 5

BREAKFAST

Summer fruit muesli (see recipe on page 57)

LUNCH

Mixed bean salad with mustard vinaigrette (see recipe on page 76)

Plain soya yoghurt

EVENING MEAL

Calabrian pasta (see recipe on page 86)

Peach and raspberry fool (see recipe on page 115)

BREAKFAST

Plate of fresh fruit, e.g. peaches, strawberries, kiwi fruit

1–2 tablespoons (15–30ml) toasted almonds, hazelnuts or cashews

LUNCH

Rice salad with apricots and pine nuts (see recipe on page 75)

EVENING MEAL

Roasted tomato salad with olives and basil (see recipe on page 80)

Boiled new potatoes with mint leaves

Plate of fresh fruit, e.g. sliced pineapple or mango

day 7

BREAKFAST

Muesli with toasted nuts and seeds (see recipe on page 58)

LUNCH

Gazpacho (see recipe on page 90)

Fresh fruit e.g. pineapple, mango or papaya

EVENING MEAL

Aromatic herb salad with asparagus and avocado (see recipe on page 73)

Cooked millet or quinoa mixed with toasted pine nuts

day 8

BREAKFAST

Slice of rye (or other non-wheat) bread with a little honey

Fresh fruit, e.g. grapes, melon, grapefruit

LUNCH

Bean sprout salad with dates and ginger dressing (see recipe on page 68)

Plain soya yoghurt (shop-bought or see recipe on page 60) with fresh fruit

EVENING MEAL

Baked sweet potato with a drizzle of extra virgin olive oil or flaxseed oil

1–2 tablespoons (15–30ml) guacamole (see recipe on page 104)

Mixed salad leaves

BREAKFAST

Plain soya yoghurt (shop-bought or see recipe on page 60)

Bowl of fresh fruit, e.g. raspberries, strawberries, blueberries

LUNCH

Slice of rye (or non-wheat) bread

Tomato salsa (see recipe page 101)

1–2 tablespoons (15–30ml) toasted nuts or seeds

EVENING MEAL

Watercress and avocado salad (see recipe on page 63)

Strawberry mousse (see recipe on page 114)

day 10

BREAKFAST

Banana tofu shake (see recipe on page 137)

LUNCH

Grilled vegetable bruschetta (see recipe on page 87)

Plate of fresh fruit, e.g. strawberries, raspberries, blueberries

EVENING MEAL

Summer risotto with spinach (see recipe on page 85)

Half a cantaloupe or galia melon

day 11

BREAKFAST

Summer fruit muesli (see recipe on page 57)

LUNCH

Slice of rye (or non-wheat) bread

Guacamole (see recipe on page 104)

Crudités, e.g. carrot, cucumber, red pepper, cherry tomatoes, celery

Fresh fruit, e.g. nectarines or peaches

EVENING MEAL

Roasted peppers with millet and cashew nuts (see recipe on page 83)

day 12

BREAKFAST

Summer berry detox juice (see recipe on page 121)

LUNCH

Spicy chickpea salad (see recipe on page 78)

Plate of fresh fruit, e.g. mango or apricots

EVENING MEAL

Vegetable kebabs (see recipe on page 89)

Cooked whole-grain rice mixed with chopped walnuts

day 13

BREAKFAST

Raisin and cinnamon oat porridge (see recipe on page 59)

LUNCH

Watercress and avocado salad (see recipe on page 63)

Plate of fresh fruit, e.g. apricots, melon, grapes

EVENING MEAL

Summer vegetable soup (see recipe on page 93)

Slice of rye (or non-wheat) bread

Summer berries, e.g. strawberries, raspberries or blueberries
with tofu 'cream' (see recipe on page 118), (if liked)

day 14

BREAKFAST

Super-charge juice (see recipe on page 127)

1–2 tablespoons (15–30ml) toasted pumpkin and sunflower seeds

LUNCH

Rye crackers or oatcakes

Hummus (see recipe on page 103)

Crudités, e.g. carrot, cucumber, red pepper, cherry tomatoes, celery

Green and red fruit (see recipe on page 107)

EVENING MEAL

Warm salad of green beans with cashews (see recipe on page 81)

Cooked whole-grain rice, quinoa or millet

Rhubarb and strawberry compote (see recipe on page 111)

menus for entertaining

SUMMER MENU 1

FIRST COURSE
Grilled vegetable bruschetta (see recipe page 87)

MAIN COURSE
Roasted peppers with millet and cashew nuts (see recipe on page 83)
Lamb's lettuce salad with walnuts (see recipe on page 65)

DESSERT
Grilled fruit kebabs with honey glaze (see recipe on page 112)

SUMMER MENU 2

FIRST COURSE
Chargrilled aubergine salad with honey dressing and hazelnuts
(see recipe on page 74)

MAIN COURSE
Oven-baked falafel with tomato salsa (see recipe on page 84)
Rocket and watercress salad with pumpkin seeds (see recipe on page 66)
New potatoes with mint leaves

DESSERT
Summer fruits jelly (see recipe on page 109)

SUMMER MENU 3

FIRST COURSE
Asparagus salad with olives and hazelnuts (see recipe on page 79)

MAIN COURSE
Summer risotto with spinach (see recipe on page 85)
Mixed salad leaves with fresh herb dressing (see recipe on page 97)

DESSERT
Summer fruits crumble (see recipe on page 113)

CHAPTER 9
BREAKFASTS

OATS ARE THE PERFECT BREAKFAST FOOD AS THEY PROVIDE YOU WITH A SUSTAINED RELEASE OF ENERGY. THEY CAN ALSO HELP TO LOWER BLOOD CHOLESTEROL LEVELS AND ARE A GOOD SOURCE OF SOLUBLE FIBRE, MAGNESIUM AND ZINC. SOAKING THE OATS IN MILK OVERNIGHT MAKES THEM SOFTER AND EASIER TO EAT. IN THIS RECIPE, THEY ARE MIXED WITH HEART-HEALTHY LINSEEDS AND VITAMIN C-PACKED SUMMER BERRIES.

SUMMER FRUIT MUESLI

MAKES 4 SERVINGS

175 g (6 oz) oats

300 ml (1/2 pint) soya, rice, almond or oat 'milk'

2 tablespoons (30 ml) sultanas

2 tablespoons (30 ml) toasted flaked almonds, chopped hazelnuts or cashews

2 tablespoons (30 ml) linseeds (ground)

225 g (8 oz) berry fruits, e.g. blueberries, blackberries, strawberries, raspberries

1 apple, peeled and grated

In a large bowl, mix together the oats, milk, sultanas, nuts and ground linseeds. Cover and leave overnight (or up to 3 days) in the fridge.

To serve, stir in the berry fruits and grated apple. Spoon into cereal bowls.

muesli with
toasted nuts seeds

THIS RECIPE IS THE PERFECT
BASE FOR ADDING
NUTRIENT-PACKED NUTS
AND SEEDS TO YOUR DAILY
DIET. TRY USING MILLET
FLAKES; THEY ARE RICHER
IN PROTEIN AND IRON THAN
OTHER GRAINS.

MUESLI WITH TOASTED NUTS AND SEEDS
MAKES 4 SERVINGS

175–200 g (6–7oz) millet or rice flakes

300ml (½ pint) chilled fruit juice or rice,

soya, almond or oat 'milk'

2 tablespoons (30 ml) sunflower seeds, lightly toasted

2 tablespoons (30 ml) pumpkin seeds, lightly toasted

60 g (2 oz) toasted flaked almonds

60 g (2 oz) chopped toasted hazelnuts

60 g (1 oz) raisins or sultanas

Fresh fruit, e.g. grated apple, sliced banana,

strawberries (optional)

Put the cereal flakes in a bowl and pour the juice or milk
over them. Leave to soak for 15 minutes.

Add the seeds, nuts and raisins and mix the ingredients
together. Serve in individual bowls, topped with the fresh
fruit (if liked).

RAISIN AND CINNAMON OAT PORRIDGE

MAKES 4 SERVINGS

175 g (6oz) porridge oats

250 ml (9 fl oz) rice, sesame or almond milk

250 ml (9 fl oz) water

1–2 tablespoons (15–30 ml) linseed (flaxseed) oil

1 teaspoon (5 ml) cinnamon

4 tablespoons (60 ml) raisins

2 tablespoons (30 ml) chopped toasted almonds

Mix the oats, milk and water in a saucepan. Bring to the boil and cook for about 5 minutes, stirring frequently.

Stir in the linseed (flaxseed) oil, cinnamon, raisins and nuts. Serve immediately while still warm.

raisin and cinnamon oat porridge

MAKING YOUR OWN
YOGHURT IS FAR EASIER
THAN YOU MIGHT IMAGINE.
IT'S NUTRITIOUS AND,
UNLIKE MOST SHOP-
BOUGHT BRANDS,
IS NOT LOADED WITH
SUGAR AND ARTIFICIAL
ADDITIVES. SOYA IS
RICH IN PROTEIN AND
CALCIUM AND A REGULAR
DAILY INTAKE CAN HELP
PROTECT AGAINST
BREAST CANCER.

HOME-MADE SOYA YOGHURT WITH FRUIT

600 ml (1 pint) soya milk

1 tablespoon (15 ml) live natural soya yoghurt

4 tablespoons (60 ml) soya milk powder (optional)

3 tablespoons (45 ml) puréed fresh fruit, pure fruit compote or fruit spread

Heat the soya milk in a saucepan until it reaches boiling point. Remove from the heat and allow to cool.

When tepid, mix in the soya yoghurt and soya milk powder.

Pour into a clean vacuum flask or yoghurt maker. Place the vacuum flask in a warm place for about 8 hours or overnight. Pour out into a clean bowl and place in the fridge until firm.

Stir in the puréed fruit, fruit compote or spread.

TOASTED PINEAPPLE AND PEACHES

MAKES 4 SERVINGS

8 slices fresh pineapple, trimmed and core removed

4 peaches, skinned and halved

1 tablespoon (15 ml) sweet almond oil

60 g (2 oz) flaked toasted almonds

LIGHTLY TOASTED FRESH FRUIT MAKES A WELCOME CHANGE FROM CEREAL AT BREAKFAST TIME. THE ALMONDS ADD PROTEIN AND CALCIUM.

Pre-heat a hot grill.

Arrange the fruit, cut side uppermost, on a foil-lined grill tray. Brush the cut sides with the almond oil. Grill for 2–3 minutes.

Arrange the toasted fruit on individual plates then sprinkle over the almond flakes. Serve.

toasted pineapple and peaches

CHAPTER 10
SALADS

WATERCRESS AND AVOCADO SALAD
MAKES 4 SERVINGS

1 bunch of watercress, washed well

1 avocado

2 or 3 spring onions

2 tablespoons (30 ml) extra virgin olive oil

1 tablespoon (15 ml) lemon juice

1 clove of garlic, finely chopped

Pick off any very thick stalks from the watercress.

Cut the avocado into quarters, remove the stone and then peel carefully. Slice lengthways.

Trim and coarsely chop the spring onions.

Combine the watercress, avocado and spring onions in a large bowl.

Shake the olive oil, lemon juice and garlic in a bottle or screw-top glass jar then drizzle over the salad. Toss lightly then serve.

watercress and avocado salad

ALL CABBAGES ARE HIGH IN FIBRE, VITAMIN C, BETACAROTENE AND CANCER-PROTECTIVE NUTRIENTS CALLED GLUCOSINOLATES. THEY ARE GREAT 'CLEANSERS', HELPING THE LIVER TO WORK PROPERLY AND DETOXIFY.

RED COLESLAW
MAKES 4 SERVINGS

Quarter of a white cabbage

Quarter of a red cabbage

1 large carrot

1 apple

60 g (2 oz) raisins

30 g (1 oz) chopped roast hazelnuts

4 tablespoons (60 ml) tofu mayonnaise

(see recipe on page 98)

Finely shred the cabbages.

Scrape or peel and grate the carrot. Grate the apple.

Mix the cabbage, carrot and apple then add the raisins and hazelnuts.

Combine the tofu mayonnaise with the salad and serve.

red coleslaw

LAMB'S LETTUCE SALAD WITH WALNUTS

MAKES 4 SERVINGS

1 pack (85 g) of ready-washed lamb's lettuce

Approximately 125 g (4 oz) ready-washed
baby spinach leaves

2 tablespoons (30 ml) extra virgin olive oil

1 tablespoon (15 ml) walnut oil

1 tablespoon (15 ml) lemon juice

2 oranges

Place the leaves in a large salad bowl.

Place the extra virgin olive oil, walnut oil and lemon
juice in a bottle or screw-top jar and shake together
thoroughly. Pour over the salad leaves then toss so
that every leaf is well coated with the dressing.

Peel the oranges, removing as much pith as you can,
and slice thinly. Arrange the oranges in an attractive
layer over the salad leaves. Serve.

BOTH LAMB'S LETTUCE AND
SPINACH ARE BURSTING
WITH IRON, BETACAROTENE
AND FOLIC ACID. LAMB'S
LETTUCE IS ALSO RICH IN
QUERCETIN, A POWERFUL
ANTIOXIDANT THAT CAN
PROTECT AGAINST CANCER.

rocket and
watercress salad

ROCKET AND WATERCRESS SALAD WITH PUMPKIN SEEDS

MAKES 4 SERVINGS

2 tablespoons (30 ml) pumpkin seeds

Half the quantity of the honey and mustard dressing

(see recipe on page 96)

1 packet (85 g) ready-washed rocket

1 packet (100 g) of ready-washed watercress

Approximately 85 g (3 oz) black and white seedless grapes

About 12 radishes

PUMPKIN SEEDS ARE RICH IN OMEGA-3 OILS AS WELL AS ZINC, VITAMIN E AND MAGNESIUM – ALL HEART-HEALTHY NUTRIENTS. TOASTING THEM, AS IN THIS RECIPE, BRINGS OUT THEIR FLAVOUR.

Lightly toast the pumpkin seeds under a hot grill for about 5 minutes until they start to turn slightly brown and emit a wonderful nutty aroma. Allow to cool.

Meanwhile, combine the rocket and watercress in a large salad bowl. Drizzle over the dressing then toss until all of the leaves are coated with the dressing.

Wash and halve the grapes.

Wash, trim and quarter the radishes and arrange the grapes and radishes on top of the leaves.

Scatter the toasted pumpkin seeds over the salad then serve.

with pumpkin
seeds

CHICKPEA AND CHERRY TOMATO SALAD

MAKES 4 SERVINGS

THIS PROTEIN-RICH SALAD CAN BE VARIED BY USING READY-BOUGHT MARINATED PEPPERS OR AUBERGINES INSTEAD OF THE ARTICHOKES, AND SUBSTITUTING OTHER KINDS OF FRESH HERBS FOR THE BASIL AND PARSLEY. CHICKPEAS ARE AN EXCELLENT SOURCE OF FIBRE, PROTEIN AND IRON. THEY CONTAIN FRUCTO-OLIGOSACCHARIDES, A TYPE OF FIBRE THAT MAINTAINS HEALTHY GUT FLORA.

2 x 400g (14 oz) cans of chickpeas, rinsed and drained

225 g (8 oz) marinated artichoke hearts

450 g (1 lb) cherry tomatoes, halved

Small bunch of spring onions, sliced

Handful of fresh basil leaves

Handful of fresh parsley, chopped

Freshly ground black pepper

Dressing:

3 tablespoons (45 ml) extra virgin olive oil

1 tablespoon (15 ml) lemon juice

½ teaspoon (2.5 ml) Dijon mustard

1 small clove of garlic, crushed

Put the chickpeas, artichoke hearts, cherry tomatoes and spring onions in a bowl.

Make the dressing by placing the ingredients into a screw-top glass jar and shaking well.

Pour the dressing over the salad. Add the herbs and black pepper and mix together well.

Chill and serve.

chickpea
and cherry tomato salad

BEAN SPROUTS ARE RICH IN IRON AND FIBRE AND ALSO CONTAIN SOME PROTEIN. THEY GO REALLY WELL WITH DATES – ALSO A GOOD SOURCE OF IRON – WHICH PROVIDE NATURAL SWEETNESS AND AN INTERESTING TEXTURE COMBINATION.

BEAN SPROUT SALAD WITH DATES AND GINGER DRESSING

MAKES 4 SERVINGS

1 pack (125 g) bean sprouts

Half a pack (50 g) ready-washed watercress

1 red pepper

Half a red onion

1 tablespoon (15 ml) rapeseed oil

1 tablespoon (15 ml) walnut oil

Juice of 1 lime

2.5 cm (1 in) piece fresh root ginger,

grated and juice squeezed out

Salt and pepper to taste

About 12 fresh dates (or you can use dried whole dates)

Wash and dry the bean sprouts. Mix with the watercress in a large salad bowl.

Remove the seeds from the pepper and slice finely. Slice the red onion finely. Combine the salad vegetables together.

Make the dressing by shaking the rapeseed and walnut oils, lime juice and ginger juice together in a bottle or screw-top jar. Season to taste.

Pour the dressing over the salad and toss well.

Halve the dates and remove the stones then arrange over the top of the salad. Serve.

CARROT AND ALMOND SALAD

MAKES 4 SERVINGS

4 large carrots

1 orange

1 lemon or lime

Handful (about 45 g) of raisins

3 tablespoons (45 ml) extra virgin olive oil

2 tablespoons (30 ml) toasted flaked almonds

Scrub or peel the carrots and grate them coarsely.

Scrub the orange and lemon or lime, then finely grate the rind and add it to the carrots.

Toss through the carrots then stir in the raisins.

Squeeze the orange and lemon or lime and mix the juice with the extra virgin olive oil in a screw-top jar.

Pour the dressing over the carrot salad. Scatter over the toasted flaked almonds and serve.

CARROTS ARE ONE OF THE BEST DETOXIFYING FOODS, HELPING TO CLEANSE THE BODY. AND IT'S TRUE THAT THEY CAN HELP YOU TO SEE IN THE DARK AS THEY ARE PACKED WITH BETACAROTENE, NEEDED FOR VISION IN DIM LIGHT. JUST ONE MEDIUM CARROT GIVES YOU YOUR DAILY REQUIREMENT OF BETACAROTENE.

ROASTED MEDITERRANEAN VEGETABLE SALAD

MAKES 4 SERVINGS

1 aubergine

3 courgettes

1 yellow pepper

1 red pepper

1 bulb of fennel

1 red onion

3 tablespoons (45 ml) extra virgin olive oil

2 cloves of garlic, chopped

A few sprigs of rosemary

A handful of black olives (marinated in olive oil, not in brine)

1 pack (185 g) ready-washed baby spinach

1–2 tablespoons (15–30 ml) sunflower seeds, toasted

THE AUBERGINE AND COURGETTES PROVIDE LOTS OF PHYTONUTRIENTS, THE PEPPERS GIVE YOU PLENTY OF VITAMIN C AND THE FENNEL IS A GREAT 'CLEANSER'. ADD TO THAT SOME BABY SPINACH AND HEART-HEALTHY OLIVE OIL AND YOU'VE GOT A WONDERFULLY NUTRITIOUS SALAD THAT'S GOOD-LOOKING ENOUGH TO SERVE TO DINNER GUESTS.

Pre-heat the oven to 200 C/ 400 F/ Gas mark 6.

Slice the aubergine and courgettes lengthways.

Remove the seeds from the peppers and cut them into wide strips.

Slice the fennel lengthways.

Cut the red onion into wedges.

Place all the vegetables in a large roasting tin and mix with the garlic and rosemary. Drizzle over the olive oil and toss lightly so that the vegetables are well coated in the oil.

Roast in the oven for about 30 minutes until the vegetables are slightly charred on the outside and tender in the middle. Mix with the black olives.

Arrange the baby spinach on four plates. Divide the roasted vegetables between the plates and pile on top of the spinach. Serve sprinkled with the toasted sunflower seeds.

CHICORY IS A RENOWNED
CLEANSER AND DETOXIFIER.
IT ALSO PROVIDES VITAMIN
C AND BETACAROTENE. ITS
BITTER TASTE IS COMPLEMENTED
PERFECTLY IN THIS SALAD WITH
THE NATURAL SWEETNESS
OF THE ORANGES AND DATES.
FINALLY, THE WALNUTS PROVIDE
PROTEIN AND VITAMIN E.

BITTERSWEET SALAD
MAKES 4 SERVINGS

1 frisee lettuce

2 bulbs of chicory

1 orange

Half the quantity of the honey and mustard dressing

(see recipe on page 96)

About 8 whole dates

60 g (2 oz) walnuts, chopped

Separate, wash and dry the frisee lettuce.

Separate, wash and chop the chicory leaves
into bite-sized pieces.

Place the leaves in a large bowl.

Peel the oranges, removing as much pith as you can,
and slice thinly. Add to the salad leaves.

Pour over the dressing and toss the salad well so that
everything is well coated.

Halve the dates and arrange on the top. Scatter over
the walnuts then serve.

bittersweet salad

PUY LENTIL AND TOMATO SALAD WITH WALNUTS

MAKES 4 SERVINGS

225 g (8 oz) Puy lentils

(or 2 x 400 g cans brown lentils)

1 red onion, finely chopped

225 g (8 oz) cherry tomatoes, halved

2 tablespoons (30 ml) chopped fresh

parsley or mint

3 tablespoons (45 ml) extra virgin olive oil

1 tablespoon (15 ml) red wine vinegar

Salt and freshly ground black pepper

60 g (2 oz) walnut pieces

125 g (4 oz) pack ready-washed salad leaves

THIS MAIN COURSE SALAD PROVIDES PLENTY OF PROTEIN, FIBRE AND IRON. LENTILS ARE EXCELLENT INTESTINAL CLEANSERS.

Put the lentils in a bowl, cover with water and leave to soak for an hour. Drain.

Place in a large saucepan, cover with fresh water or vegetable stock, and bring to the boil. Reduce the heat and simmer for about an hour or until tender. Drain.

Transfer to a bowl and mix with the red onion, tomatoes and chopped herbs.

Place the olive oil and red wine vinegar in a bottle or screw-top glass jar and shake together. Pour the dressing over the lentil salad.

Toss lightly and season with salt and pepper.

Arrange the salad leaves on a serving plate, pile the lentil salad on top then sprinkle with the walnuts.

This salad can be eaten warm or chilled.

AROMATIC HERB SALAD WITH ASPARAGUS AND AVOCADO

MAKES 4 SERVINGS

2 handfuls of herb leaves –

rocket, coriander, parsley, basil

2 avocados

3 tablespoons (45 ml) lemon juice

225 g (8 oz) asparagus spears

2 tablespoons (30 ml) extra virgin olive oil

1 tablespoon (15 ml) pumpkin seed oil

60 g (2 oz) toasted pumpkin seeds

Wash and dry the herbs. Place in a large salad bowl.

Cut the avocados in half, remove the stone and peel. Dice the flesh and toss immediately in 2 tablespoons (30 ml) of the lemon juice to prevent it from going brown.

Trim the asparagus spears. Steam for 3 minutes so they are still quite firm. Drain and allow them to cool.

Remove the avocado from the lemon juice and add to the herbs with the asparagus spears and pumpkin seeds.

Shake the extra virgin olive oil, pumpkin seed oil and the remaining 1 tablespoon (15 ml) of lemon juice in a bottle or screw-top glass jar. Drizzle this dressing over the salad. Toss well then serve.

FRESH HERBS ARE PLENTIFUL IN THE SUMMER AND ARE RICH IN BETACAROTENE, IRON AND VITAMIN C.

asparagus

AUBERGINES ARE BEST EATEN CHARGRILLED OR OVEN-ROASTED, TO MINIMISE THE NEED FOR ADDED OIL AND TO RETAIN THE NUTRIENTS. THEY ARE A GOOD SOURCE OF FOLIC ACID AND POTASSIUM.

CHARGRILLED AUBERGINE SALAD WITH HONEY DRESSING AND HAZELNUTS
MAKES 4 SERVINGS

1 aubergine

2 tablespoons (30 ml) extra virgin olive oil

125 g (4 oz) plum tomatoes

1 large pack (185 g) ready-washed salad leaves

60 g (2 oz) toasted chopped hazelnuts

1 tablespoon (15 ml) basil leaves, torn

Dressing:

2 tablespoons (30 ml) extra virgin olive oil

2 teaspoons (10 ml) lemon juice

1/2 teaspoon (2.5 ml) clear honey

Sea salt and freshly ground black pepper

Cut the aubergine into thin slices, brush with olive oil and place on a foil-lined tray. Cook under a hot grill for 2–3 minutes each side until slightly charred and softened. Allow to cool.

Thinly slice the plum tomatoes.

Place the salad leaves in a large salad bowl. Add the aubergine, tomatoes and hazelnuts.

To make the dressing, place the olive oil, lemon juice, honey, salt and pepper in a screw-top glass jar and shake well until mixed. Pour the dressing over the salad, toss well and scatter over the torn basil leaves. Serve.

aubergine salad

WHOLE-GRAIN (BROWN) RICE LITERALLY IS THE WHOLE OF THE RICE GRAIN, INCLUDING THE SURROUNDING BRAN LAYERS, WHICH CONTAIN THE FIBRE, MAGNESIUM, PHOSPHORUS, THIAMIN (VITAMIN B1) AND IRON, WHICH ARE NECESSARY IN OUR DIET. IT MAKES A DELICIOUS BASE FOR SUMMER SALADS, AND ITS NUTTY FLAVOUR IS PERFECTLY COMPLEMENTED BY DRIED FRUIT AND TOASTED NUTS. TO SAVE TIME, TRY THE PARBOILED VARIETY, WHICH TAKES ONLY 10 MINUTES TO COOK.

rice salad

RICE SALAD WITH APRICOTS AND PINE NUTS

MAKES 4 SERVINGS

225 g (8 oz) whole-grain (brown) rice

2 tablespoons (30 ml) extra virgin olive oil

1 onion, peeled and chopped

2 cloves of garlic, crushed

60 g (2 oz) flaked almonds

60 g (2 oz) pine nuts

1 tablespoon (15 ml) lemon juice

85 g (3 oz) ready-to-eat dried apricots

2 tablespoons (30 ml) chopped fresh coriander

Bring a large pan of water to the boil. Stir in the rice. Cover and simmer for the time recommended on the packet. Drain. Alternatively, cook the rice in twice its own volume of water until the water has been absorbed.

Meanwhile, heat the olive oil in a pan, add the onion and garlic and cook over a moderate heat for 5 minutes until they are translucent. Turn up the heat, add the almonds and pine nuts and cook for a few minutes longer, stirring often, until the onion and nuts are golden brown.

Add the onion mixture to the rice, along with the lemon juice, the apricots and coriander.

Mix together then transfer to a serving dish.

mixed bean salad with
mustard
vinaigrette

THIS PULSE SALAD IS A
GREAT WAY OF BOOSTING
YOUR PROTEIN INTAKE.
BEANS ALSO PROVIDE
SOLUBLE FIBRE, WHICH
IS GREAT FOR CLEANSING
THE DIGESTIVE SYSTEM,
AS WELL AS B VITAMINS,
IRON AND ZINC. YOU
CAN SUBSTITUTE OTHER
VARIETIES OF COOKED
BEANS FOR THE ONES
SUGGESTED IN
THIS RECIPE.

MIXED BEAN SALAD WITH MUSTARD VINAIGRETTE

MAKES 4 SERVINGS

85 g (3 oz) green beans, trimmed and halved

225 g (8 oz) can red kidney beans, drained

225 g (8 oz) can butter beans, drained

225 g (8 oz) can flageolet beans, drained

60 g (2 oz) button mushrooms, sliced

2 tablespoons (30 ml) extra virgin olive oil

1 teaspoon (5 ml) whole-grain mustard

1 teaspoon (5 ml) clear honey

2 teaspoons (10 ml) cider vinegar

1 tablespoon (15 ml) fresh parsley, chopped

Steam the green beans for 4–5 minutes. Drain and refresh under cold running water.

Place the canned beans, green beans and mushrooms in a large bowl and mix together.

Put the olive oil, mustard, honey, vinegar and parsley in a screw-top glass jar, shake well and pour the dressing over the salad.

Toss lightly and serve. This salad can be kept in the fridge for up to two days.

THIS SALAD IS QUICK TO PREPARE AND MAKES A DELICIOUS MIDWEEK LUNCH. WALNUTS ARE PARTICULARLY RICH IN OMEGA-3 FATTY ACIDS, WHICH HELP LOWER THE RISK OF HEART ATTACKS AND STROKE AS WELL AS REDUCE JOINT STIFFNESS.

ORIENTAL SALAD WITH WALNUTS

MAKES 4 SERVINGS

225 g (8 oz) bean sprouts

1 red pepper, deseeded and diced

60 g (2 oz) mushrooms, sliced

6 spring onions, cut into 2.5 cm (1 in) lengths

125 g (4 oz) baby corn

85 g (3 oz) pack ready-washed watercress

85 g (3 oz) walnuts, roughly chopped

3 tablespoons (45 ml) extra virgin olive oil

2 teaspoons (10 ml) clear honey

1 tablespoon (15 ml) cider vinegar

1 teaspoon (5 ml) light soy sauce or tamarind

1 clove of garlic, crushed

1 thin slice of fresh ginger, peeled and finely chopped

Place the bean sprouts, red pepper, mushrooms, spring onions, baby corn and watercress in a salad bowl and mix together. Add the walnuts.

To make the dressing, put the remaining ingredients in a screw-top glass jar and shake well. Pour the dressing over the salad and toss lightly. Serve.

oriental salad with walnuts

SPICY CHICKPEA SALAD

MAKES 4 SERVINGS

175 g (6 oz) mangetout, trimmed and cut into halves

Half a small red onion, finely chopped

2 x 400g (14 oz) cans of chickpeas,
rinsed and drained

1 pack (150–185 g) ready-washed
mixed salad leaves

Dressing:

2 tablespoons (30 ml) rapeseed oil

1 teaspoon (5 ml) ground cumin

Pinch ground cinnamon

Pinch ground cloves

Sea salt and pepper

THIS SALAD PROVIDES LOTS OF PROTEIN, IRON, MAGNESIUM AND B VITAMINS. CHICKPEAS ARE RICH IN SOLUBLE FIBRE AND HELP IMPROVE THE NORMAL FUNCTIONING OF THE DIGESTIVE SYSTEM.

Steam the mangetout over boiling water for 2 minutes then allow to cool.

Put the chopped onion, chickpeas and mangetout in a serving bowl.

Make the dressing by putting the oil, spices and seasoning in a screw-top glass jar and shake well. Pour over the chickpea salad and combine together.

Arrange the salad leaves on a serving dish. Pile on the chickpea salad and serve.

spicy chickpea salad

asparagus
salad

IF YOU NEED AN IMMUNITY BOOST OR HAVE RECENTLY TAKEN A COURSE OF ANTIBIOTICS, ASPARAGUS COULD BE THE KEY TO GETTING YOUR HEALTH BACK ON TRACK. AS WELL AS TASTING DELICIOUS IT CONTAINS FRUCTO-OLIGOSACCHARIDES, A TYPE OF FIBRE THAT RESTORES LEVELS OF HEALTHY GUT BACTERIA. IT IS ALSO A NATURAL DIURETIC AND CAN RELIEVE FLUID RETENTION. FIVE ASPARAGUS SPEARS GIVE YOU HALF OF YOUR DAILY FOLIC ACID NEEDS.

ASPARAGUS SALAD WITH OLIVES AND HAZELNUTS

MAKES 4 SERVINGS

225 g (8 oz) asparagus spears

125 g (4 oz) baby spinach or rocket leaves

450 g (1 lb) vine-ripened tomatoes, sliced

2 tablespoons (30 ml) extra virgin olive oil

1 tablespoon (15 ml) balsamic vinegar

45 g (1½ oz) black olives

45 g (1½ oz) toasted chopped hazelnuts

Steam the asparagus for 6–8 minutes. Refresh under cold running water and then cut into 5 cm (2 in) lengths.

Arrange the leaves on a serving plate. Arrange the asparagus and tomato slices on top of the leaves.

To make the dressing, put the oil and vinegar in a screw-top glass jar and shake well.

Drizzle over the salad. Scatter over the olives and hazelnuts and serve.

ROASTING TOMATOES
BRINGS OUT THEIR
NATURAL SWEETNESS
AND INTENSIFIES THEIR
FLAVOUR. THEY RETAIN
ALL OF THEIR LYCOPENE
(A POWERFUL ANTIOXIDANT)
AND MUCH OF THEIR
VITAMIN C, AS THEY ARE
COOKED IN OIL RATHER
THAN WATER.

ROASTED TOMATO SALAD WITH OLIVES AND BASIL

MAKES 4 SERVINGS

8 large plum tomatoes

2 cloves of garlic, finely chopped

A little sea salt and freshly ground black pepper

15–20 black olives

A handful of fresh basil leaves

2 tablespoons (30 ml) extra virgin olive oil

1 pack (100 g) ready-washed rocket leaves

Pre-heat the oven to 200 C/ 400 F/ Gas mark 6.

Cut the tomatoes into halves and place in a roasting tin, cut side up. Scatter over the chopped garlic, sea salt and black pepper, olives and basil leaves.

Drizzle over the olive oil, turning the tomatoes gently so that each one is coated in a little oil.

Cook in the oven for 45–50 minutes. Allow to cool then serve with the rocket leaves.

roasted tomato salad with olives and basil

YOUNG GREEN BEANS FORM THE CENTRAL PART OF THIS SALAD. THEY ARE A GOOD SOURCE OF IRON, FOLIC ACID AND BETACAROTENE. THE CASHEWS SUPPLY PROTEIN, CALCIUM AND VITAMIN E.

WARM SALAD OF GREEN BEANS WITH CASHEWS

MAKES 4 SERVINGS

450 g (1 lb) thin green beans, trimmed

85 g (3 oz) cashew nuts, lightly toasted

2 tablespoons (30 ml) extra virgin olive oil

1 tablespoon (15 ml) cider or wine vinegar

1 clove of garlic, crushed

2 tablespoons (30 ml) fresh parsley, chopped

Sea salt and freshly ground black pepper

Steam the beans over boiling water for 4 minutes until they are tender-crisp. Refresh under cold running water.

Place in a bowl and mix with the toasted cashew nuts.

Place the olive oil, vinegar, garlic, parsley and seasoning in a screw-top glass jar and shake until well mixed. Drizzle over the green beans and toss lightly to combine. Serve.

warm salad of green beans with cashews

CHAPTER 11

VEGETABLES

ROASTED PEPPERS WITH MILLET AND CASHEW NUTS

MAKES 4 SERVINGS

2 large or 4 small red peppers

3 tablespoons (45 ml) extra virgin olive oil

1 small onion, chopped

2 cloves of garlic, crushed

175 g (6 oz) millet

2 tablespoons (30 ml) fresh parsley, finely chopped

600 ml (1 pint) vegetable stock

60 g (2 oz) cashew nuts, toasted

About 8 cherry tomatoes, halved

PEPPERS ARE PLENTIFUL AND CHEAP IN THE SUMMER. THEY ARE AMONG THE RICHEST SOURCES OF VITAMIN C SO NOW IS THE TIME TO BENEFIT FROM THEIR GOODNESS. ROASTING THEM IN THE OVEN BRINGS OUT THEIR SWEETNESS.

Heat the oven to 190 C/ 375 F/ Gas mark 5.

Cut the peppers in half lengthways, keeping the stalk attached, and remove the seeds. Brush the outsides with a little of the extra virgin olive oil then place them, skin-side down, in a roasting tin, packing quite tightly so they don't roll over.

Heat 2 tablespoons (30 ml) of the extra virgin olive oil in a separate pan and lightly sauté the onion for about 5 minutes until translucent. Add the millet, parsley and vegetable stock. Bring to the boil, reduce the heat then simmer for about 20 minutes or until the millet grains are soft.

Stir in the toasted cashew nuts and halved cherry tomatoes.

Spoon the millet mixture into the pepper halves. Drizzle over the remaining olive oil.

Cover the roasting tin tightly with foil and bake for 1 hour until the peppers are tender.

OVEN-BAKED FALAFEL WITH TOMATO SALSA

MAKES 12

400g (14 oz) can chickpeas, rinsed and drained

Half an onion, very finely chopped

1 tablespoon (15 ml) finely chopped fresh coriander

1 tablespoon (15 ml) finely chopped mint or parsley

2 garlic cloves, crushed

1 teaspoon (5 ml) ground coriander

1 teaspoon (5 ml) ground cumin

1 tablespoon (15 ml) gram flour (chickpea or lentil flour)

mixed with 2 tablespoons (30 ml) water

1 tablespoon (15 ml) extra virgin olive oil

Tomato Salsa:

2 large ripe tomatoes, skinned

A quarter of a red onion, finely chopped

1 tablespoon (15 ml) fresh coriander,

finely chopped

Salt and freshly ground black pepper

FALAFEL ARE PERFECT FOR AL FRESCO EATING – PICNICS, BARBECUES – AS WELL AS LUNCH ON THE MOVE. CHICKPEAS PROVIDE PROTEIN, FIBRE, IRON, MANGANESE AND MAGNESIUM. THEY INCREASE THE FRIENDLY BACTERIA OF THE GUT THAT IMPROVE DIGESTION. THESE FALAFEL ARE BAKED INSTEAD OF FRIED, SO THEY DON'T ABSORB EXTRA OIL.

Pre-heat the oven to 200 C/ 400 F/ Gas mark 6. Lightly oil a baking sheet.

Put the chickpeas in a blender or food processor and process for a few seconds.

Add the onion, coriander, mint or parsley, garlic, spices, gram flour paste and olive oil. Process for a few seconds until combined and a fairly smooth, stiff purée.

Form the mixture into balls about the size of a walnut. You should be able to make about 12. Coat lightly with a little gram flour. Place on the oiled baking sheet and cook in the pre-heated oven for about 20 minutes until golden, turning once.

Meanwhile, make the salsa:

Finely chop the tomatoes and mix with the onion and coriander. Season to taste. Chill.

Serve the cooked falafel with the salsa.

SUMMER RISOTTO WITH SPINACH

MAKES 4 SERVINGS

3 tablespoons (45 ml) extra virgin olive oil

1 onion, chopped

2 cloves of garlic, crushed

2 bay leaves

300 g (10 oz) Arborio (risotto) rice

1 litre (1¾ pints) hot vegetable stock

Large pinch saffron strands

225 g (8 oz) spinach leaves

Freshly ground black pepper

Heat the olive oil in a large heavy-based pan and cook the onion with the bay leaves and garlic over a moderate heat, stirring frequently.

Stir in the rice and cook for 1–2 minutes, stirring constantly. Add the hot vegetable stock a ladleful at a time and the saffron, stirring over a gentle heat for about 20 minutes until the rice is almost tender. Perfect risotto is creamy but not solid, and the rice should still have a little bite.

Roughly tear the spinach leaves and add to the hot risotto. Stir until the leaves have wilted. Remove the pan from the heat and season to taste with freshly ground black pepper.

SPINACH IS RICH IN IRON, MAGNESIUM, FOLIC ACID AND VITAMIN C AND IS ALSO A GREAT IMMUNE PROTECTOR. FORTUNATELY, FRESH SPINACH IS PLENTIFUL DURING THE SPRING AND SUMMER MONTHS SO MAKE THE MOST OF IT WITH THIS DELICIOUS RISOTTO.

SPROUTING AND PURPLE BROCCOLI ARE AVAILABLE DURING THE SPRING AND THIS SIMPLE PASTA DISH, ORIGINATING FROM ITALY, IS A TASTY WAY OF ADDING IT TO YOUR DIET. ALL TYPES OF BROCCOLI CONTAIN A POWERFUL ANTI-CANCER COMPOUND CALLED SULPHORAPHANE – SEVERAL STUDIES HAVE LINKED REGULAR INTAKES OF CRUCIFEROUS VEGETABLES SUCH AS BROCCOLI TO A REDUCED RISK OF CANCER OF THE BOWEL, STOMACH, BREAST AND LUNGS.

CALABRIAN PASTA
MAKES 4 SERVINGS

350 g (12 oz) non-wheat pasta

200 g (7 oz) broccoli

3 tablespoons (45 ml) extra virgin olive oil

4–6 spring onions

2 cloves of garlic, crushed

30 g (1 oz) pine nuts

60 g (2 oz) sultanas

Sea salt and freshly ground black pepper

3 tablespoons (45 ml) fresh parsley, chopped

Cook the pasta in a large pan of boiling water according to the directions on the packet.

Meanwhile, divide the broccoli heads into florets then blanch in boiling water for 1 minute. Refresh under cold running water and drain well.

Cut the spring onion into 5 cm (2 in) lengths.

Heat the olive oil in a pan and cook the spring onions, garlic and pine nuts for 30 seconds until the pine nuts start to turn golden.

Drain the pasta. Mix with the spring onion mixture, broccoli florets and sultanas. Season with a little sea salt and freshly ground black pepper to taste.

Transfer onto a serving dish and scatter over the chopped parsley. Serve warm or cold.

GRILLED VEGETABLE BRUSCHETTA

MAKES 4 SERVINGS

1 red pepper

1 yellow pepper

2 small courgettes, thinly sliced lengthways

1 red onion, thinly sliced

4 plum tomatoes, halved

45 g (1½ oz) rocket leaves

1 clove of garlic (optional)

4 slices of non-wheat bread

2 tablespoons (30 ml) extra virgin olive oil or
fresh herb dressing (see recipe on page 97)

Handful of fresh basil leaves

THIS GLORIOUS MIXTURE OF COLOURFUL SUMMER VEGETABLES IS BRIMMING WITH VITAMIN C AND ANTIOXIDANTS. IT IS DELICIOUS PILED ONTO TOASTED ROUNDS OF NON-WHEAT BREAD. TRY A LIGHT RYE BREAD OR ANY NON-WHEAT LOAF WITH A LIGHT TEXTURE.

Pre-heat the grill to high. Grill the peppers whole, turning occasionally, until blackened all over. Seal in a plastic bag and set aside to cool. Remove the skins, halve, remove the core and seeds and cut each half into three strips.

Meanwhile, arrange the courgettes, onion and tomato halves in a single layer on a grill pan. Brush with a little of the olive oil and grill for 2 minutes on each side.

If using garlic, cut the clove in half and rub the cut surface over one side of each bread slice. Toast the bread under the grill.

Pile the grilled vegetables on top of each grilled bread slice. Drizzle over the remaining olive oil or Fresh Herb Dressing and garnish with the basil leaves.

vegetable bruschetta

THIS DELICIOUS
PROVENÇAL VEGETABLE
DISH IS PACKED WITH
POWERFUL ANTIOXIDANTS,
INCLUDING VITAMIN C
(IN THE PEPPERS), NASUIN
(IN THE AUBERGINES) AND
QUERCETIN (IN THE ONIONS).
TOGETHER THEY MAKE
A POTENT ANTI-CANCER
COCKTAIL OF NUTRIENTS.

RATATOUILLE
MAKES 4 SERVINGS

3 tablespoons (45 ml) extra virgin olive oil

2 onions, peeled and chopped

1 each of red, yellow and green peppers,

deseeded and sliced

2 cloves of garlic, crushed

2 large courgettes, sliced

1 large aubergine, diced

700 g (1 1/2 lb) tomatoes, skinned and chopped

(or use 400 g/ 14 oz can tomatoes)

Sea salt and freshly ground black pepper

2 tablespoons (30 ml) chopped fresh parsley

Heat the oil in a large saucepan. Add the onions and peppers and cook gently for 5 minutes.

Add the garlic, courgettes, aubergines and tomatoes. Stir then cover and cook over a low heat for 20–25 minutes until all the vegetables are tender.

Season to taste with salt and freshly ground black pepper and sprinkle with the chopped parsley. Serve hot or cold.

VEGETABLE KEBABS

MAKES 4 SERVINGS

350 g (12 oz) firm tofu

1 red pepper, deseeded and
cut into 2.5 cm (1 in) pieces

1 yellow pepper, deseeded and
cut into 2.5 cm (1 in) pieces

2 courgettes, cut into bite-sized pieces

Half an aubergine, cut into bite-sized pieces

16 button mushrooms

8 cherry tomatoes

Marinade:

4 tablespoons (60 ml) extra virgin olive oil

1 tablespoon (15 ml) soy sauce

Grated zest and juice of 1 lime (or lemon)

1/2 teaspoon (2.5 ml) grated fresh root ginger

2 teaspoons (10 ml) clear honey

1 clove of garlic, crushed

3 tablespoons (45 ml) water

THESE KEBABS ARE PERFECT FOR AL FRESCO DINING AND BARBECUES. AS THE VEGETABLES ARE COOKED ONLY BRIEFLY AND OVER A HIGH HEAT, THEY RETAIN MOST OF THEIR NUTRIENTS. YOU CAN ALSO USE OTHER SUMMER VEGETABLES, SUCH AS PIECES OF CORN ON THE COB AND SLICES OF FENNEL.

Cut the tofu into 12 cubes. Place in a shallow dish along with the prepared vegetables.

To make the marinade, mix together the olive oil, soy sauce, lime (or lemon) juice, ginger, honey, garlic and water.

Spoon the marinade over the tofu and vegetables, making sure they are thoroughly coated. Leave for at least one hour, turning occasionally.

Thread the tofu and vegetable onto 8 bamboo skewers . Brush with the remaining marinade and place under a hot grill or on a barbecue for about 10 minutes, turning frequently and brushing with marinade, until slightly browned.

Serve hot with salad leaves.

AS THIS SOUP IS NOT COOKED, THE TOMATOES RETAIN ALL OF THEIR VITAMIN C. IT IS WONDERFULLY REFRESHING IN HOT WEATHER AND PACKED WITH FLAVOUR AND VITALITY.

GAZPACHO
MAKES 4 SERVINGS

450 g (1 lb) ripe tomatoes, skinned, deseeded and chopped

Half a cucumber, peeled, deseeded and roughly chopped

Half a green pepper, deseeded and chopped

Half a red pepper, deseeded and chopped

Half a red onion, chopped

2 cloves of garlic, crushed

3 tablespoons (45 ml) extra virgin olive oil

300 ml (1/2 pint) tomato juice

3 tablespoons (45 ml) white wine vinegar

Salt and freshly ground black pepper to season

A few ice cubes

To garnish:
2 tablespoons (30 ml) each red and green pepper, deseeded and very finely chopped

Handful of fresh chopped parsley

gazpacho

Put all the Gazpacho ingredients except for the garnish in a blender or food processor.

Depending on the size of your appliance, you may need to process the soup in two batches. Purée the mixture until smooth.

Pour the soup in a large bowl, cover and chill in the fridge for at least an hour.

Just before serving the soup, add a few ice cubes and garnish with the finely chopped peppers and parsley.

risotto with asparagus and peas

RISOTTO WITH ASPARAGUS AND PEAS

MAKES 4 SERVINGS

3 tablespoons (45 ml) extra virgin olive oil

4 shallots, chopped (or 1 onion)

300 g (10 oz) Arborio (risotto) rice

1 litre (1³/₄ pints) hot vegetable stock

350 g (12 oz) asparagus, cut into 4 cm (1¹/₂ in) lengths

125 g (4 oz) fresh or frozen peas

Finely grated zest of one lemon

Handful of fresh basil leaves, torn

Sea salt and black pepper

Heat the olive oil in a large pan. Add the shallots and cook for 2 minutes until translucent.

Add the rice and stir with a wooden spoon until the grains are coated with the oil. Add the hot vegetable stock one ladle at a time, stirring and simmer for about 10 minutes.

Add the asparagus, peas and lemon zest. Continue cooking for a further 10 minutes until all the liquid has been absorbed and the rice is tender but firm in the centre.

Stir in the basil leaves and season to taste. Serve immediately.

THIS RECIPE IS A DELICIOUS MEDLEY OF YOUNG, CRISP SUMMER VEGETABLES. COOK THEM FOR ONLY THE BRIEFEST TIME TO RETAIN THEIR CRISPNESS AND KEEP THE VITAMINS IN. QUINOA IS A NUTTY-TASTING GRAIN, RICH IN FIBRE, IRON AND MAGNESIUM AND HIGHER IN PROTEIN THAN OTHER GRAINS. YOU MAY SUBSTITUTE OTHER GRAINS, SUCH AS WHOLE-GRAIN (BROWN) RICE, BUCKWHEAT OR MILLET IF YOU PREFER.

SUMMER VEGETABLES WITH QUINOA
MAKES 4 SERVINGS

600 ml (1 pint) vegetable stock
225 g (8 oz) quinoa
175 g (6 oz) young fresh (or frozen) broad beans
125 g (4 oz) baby carrots, topped and trimmed
125 g (4 oz) sugar-snap peas, trimmed
4 tiny courgettes, halved
30 g (1 oz) pine nuts, lightly toasted

Dressing:
3 tablespoons (45 ml) extra virgin olive oil
Grated zest and juice of 1 lemon
1 tablespoon (15 ml) each of fresh mint
and coriander, chopped

Bring the vegetable stock to the boil in a large saucepan. Add the quinoa, cover and simmer for about 20 minutes until the grains are tender and the stock has been absorbed.

Steam the broad beans, whole baby carrots, sugar-snap peas and courgettes over boiling water for 4–5 minutes until just tender. Drain.

Make the dressing by placing the olive oil, lemon zest and juice and herbs in a screw-top glass jar and shaking vigorously to combine the ingredients.

Mix all the vegetables together in a pan, add the dressing and toss until the vegetables are well coated.

Spoon the vegetables on top of the quinoa. Scatter over the toasted pine nuts and serve.

THIS SOUP IS PACKED
WITH BETACAROTENE,
VITAMIN C AND MANY OTHER
ANTIOXIDANTS. AS THERE
IS NO NEED FOR COOKING,
IT RETAINS ALL THE
NUTRIENTS. VARY THE
INGREDIENTS ACCORDING
TO WHICH VEGETABLES
YOU HAVE TO HAND.

SUMMER VEGETABLE SOUP
MAKES 4 SERVINGS

6 ripe tomatoes, skinned, deseeded and chopped

Half a yellow pepper, deseeded and chopped

Half a red pepper, deseeded and chopped

125 g (4 oz) fresh young spinach leaves

Half a red onion, chopped

2 cloves of garlic, crushed

2 tablespoons (30 ml) linseed (flax) oil

300 ml (1/2 pint) carrot juice

1 cm (1/2 in) piece fresh ginger

1 tablespoon (15 ml) cider vinegar

Salt and freshly ground black pepper to season

A few ice cubes

To garnish:

Handful of fresh chopped parsley

Put all the ingredients except for the garnish and
ice cubes in a blender or food processor. Purée the
mixture until you have a smooth soup.

Pour the soup in a large bowl with the ice cubes,
cover and chill in the fridge for at least an hour.

Just before serving the soup, garnish it with the
chopped parsley.

STIR-FRYING IS A HEALTHY METHOD OF COOKING AS THE VEGETABLES ARE COOKED VERY QUICKLY AT A HIGH TEMPERATURE, WHICH RESULTS IN MUCH SMALLER LOSSES OF VITAMINS COMPARED WITH OTHER METHODS. THIS COLOURFUL COMBINATION OF SUMMER VEGETABLES CAN BE VARIED ACCORDING TO WHAT YOU HAVE AVAILABLE.

STIR-FRIED SUMMER VEGETABLES

MAKES 4 SERVINGS

1 tablespoon (15 ml) rapeseed oil

85 g (3 oz) baby carrots, trimmed

85 g (3 oz) thin green beans, trimmed

85 g (3 oz) asparagus spears,
cut into 5 cm (2 in) lengths

2 cloves of garlic, chopped

85 g (3 oz) mangetout, trimmed

2 courgettes, sliced

2 tablespoons (30 ml) orange juice

2 tablespoons (30 ml) light soy sauce

2 teaspoons (10 ml) clear honey

1/2 teaspoon (2.5 ml) grated orange zest

60 g (2 oz) toasted cashew nuts

Heat the rapeseed oil in a nonstick wok or large frying pan. Add the carrots, green beans and asparagus and stir-fry for 3 minutes. Add the garlic, mangetout, courgettes, orange juice, soy sauce and honey and stir-fry for a further 2 minutes.

Add the bean sprouts and orange zest and continue stir-frying for a further minute. Mix in the cashew nuts and serve.

stir-fried
summer vegetables

CHAPTER 12
DRESSINGS

HONEY AND MUSTARD DRESSING

5 tablespoons (75 ml) extra virgin olive oil

2 tablespoons (30 ml) cider vinegar

½ teaspoon (2.5 ml) Dijon mustard

1 level teaspoon (5 ml) clear honey

Half a clove of garlic

Place all of the ingredients in a bottle or screw-top jar and shake well.

AVOCADO DRESSING

1 avocado

2 tablespoons (30 ml) fresh lemon juice

1 teaspoon (5 ml) cider vinegar

1 spring onion, roughly chopped

Peel and roughly chop the avocado. Put in a food processor or blender with the other ingredients and whiz together for a few seconds until smooth.

FRESH HERB DRESSING

125 ml (4 fl oz) extra virgin olive oil

2 tablespoons (30 ml) chopped fresh herbs: basil, parsley, mint, chives, or chervil

2 tablespoons (30 ml) good quality balsamic vinegar

1–2 teaspoons (5–10 ml) Dijon mustard

1 clove of garlic, lightly crushed

Place the fresh herbs and olive oil in a screw-top jar and shake well. Add the vinegar, mustard and garlic. Shake again.

WALNUT DRESSING

2 tablespoons (30 ml) extra virgin olive oil

1 tablespoon (15 ml) walnut oil

Juice of 1 lemon

30 g (1 oz) walnuts, lightly toasted and chopped

Mix all the ingredients together in a small bottle or screw-top jar.

THIS VERSION OF MAYONNAISE
IS MADE WITHOUT EGGS.
IT INCLUDES TOFU, WHICH IS
RICH IN PROTEIN, CALCIUM
AND SOY ISOFLAVONES,
WHICH LOWER BLOOD
CHOLESTEROL AND PROTECT
AGAINST HEART DISEASE.

TOFU MAYONNAISE

60 g (2 oz) silken tofu

Grated zest and juice of half a lemon

2 tablespoons (30 ml) rapeseed oil

2 tablespoons (30 ml) water

1 clove of garlic, crushed

1 tablespoon (15 ml) fresh coriander,

chopped (optional)

A little sea salt and freshly ground black pepper

Put all the ingredients except the coriander in a food processor or blender. Blend until smooth and thick. Adjust the consistency if necessary by adding a little more water (to thin) or tofu (to thicken). Stir in the coriander and season to taste.

tofu mayonnaise

CHAPTER 13
SALADS AND DIPS

FRESH CORIANDER IS BURSTING WITH BETACAROTENE, VITAMIN C AND IRON. THIS SALSA MAKES A GREAT ACCOMPANIMENT TO GRILLED VEGETABLES AND VEGETABLE KEBABS.

CORIANDER SALSA
MAKES 4 SERVINGS

3 tablespoons (45 ml) fresh coriander, finely chopped

1 tablespoon (15 ml) flat-leaf parsley, finely chopped

225 g (8 oz) ripe plum tomatoes, skinned

Half a green chilli, deseeded and finely chopped

Half a red onion, finely chopped

Sea salt to taste

Place the herbs in a bowl. Halve and remove the seeds from the tomatoes then dice finely. Add to the herbs along with the chilli and red onion. Mix well and season with a little sea salt.

Chill in the fridge for at least 2 hours.

TOMATO SALSA MAKES A
GREAT ACCOMPANIMENT
TO CRUDITÉS AND GRILLED
VEGETABLES. IT ALSO
ENLIVENS STEAMED OR
ROASTED VEGETABLES.

TOMATO SALSA

MAKES 4 SERVINGS

2 large ripe tomatoes or 4 ripe plum tomatoes,
skinned deseeded and finely diced
1–2 tablespoons (15–30 ml) chopped fresh parsley
or coriander
1 teaspoon (5 ml) finely chopped fresh chilli
(or according to your taste)
1 small clove of garlic, crushed
1 tablespoon (15 ml) olive oil
2 spring onions, finely chopped
2 tablespoons (30 ml) lemon or lime juice

Combine all of the ingredients in a bowl.

Chill in the fridge for at least 2 hours before serving.

THIS SALSA IS ESPECIALLY GOOD WITH STEAMED OR ROASTED VEGETABLES. USE IT, TOO, AS A SANDWICH FILLING WITH NON-WHEAT BREAD, OR AS A TOPPING FOR JACKET POTATOES.

CHERRY TOMATO, CORN AND AVOCADO SALSA

MAKES ABOUT 1 PINT (600 ML)

About 8 cherry tomatoes, halved or quartered (depending on the size)

225 g (8 oz) canned sweetcorn, rinsed

1 small ripe avocado, peeled and diced

1 tablespoon (15 ml) chopped fresh basil

Half a small red onion, finely diced

2 tablespoons (30 ml) extra virgin olive oil

2 tablespoons (30 ml) fresh lime juice

1 clove of garlic, crushed

Sea salt and freshly ground black pepper to taste

Put all of the ingredients in a bowl and mix together.

Chill in the fridge for at least 2 hours before serving.

ALTHOUGH HUMMUS IS WIDELY AVAILABLE IN SUPERMARKETS, IT'S WORTH MAKING YOUR OWN SO YOU CAN REDUCE THE SALT AND OIL CONTENT. THIS TASTY DIP GOES WELL IN SANDWICHES (MADE WITH NON-WHEAT BREAD) OR SPREAD ON RYE CRACKERS AND RICE CAKES.

HUMMUS
MAKES 4 SERVINGS

125 g (4 oz) chickpeas, soaked overnight

(or use a 400 g tin, drained and rinsed)

2 garlic cloves, crushed

2 tablespoons (30 ml) olive oil

120 ml (4 fl oz) tahini

Juice of 1 lemon

Pinch of paprika or cayenne pepper

Freshly ground black pepper

Drain then cook the chickpeas in plenty of water for about 60–90 minutes or according to directions on the packet. Drain, reserving the liquid.

Purée the cooked chickpeas with the remaining ingredients and enough of the cooking liquid to make a creamy consistency.

Taste and add more black pepper or lemon juice if necessary.

Chill in the fridge for at least 2 hours before serving.

guacamole

AVOCADOS ARE BRIMMING WITH HEART-HEALTHY NUTRIENTS: MONOUNSATURATED OILS, VITAMIN E, FOLIC ACID AND POTASSIUM. THIS DIP IS EASY TO MAKE AND CAN BE USED AS A SANDWICH SPREAD, A DIP FOR VEGETABLE CRUDITÉS OR FOR SPOONING ON SALADS.

GUACAMOLE (AVOCADO DIP)
MAKES 4 SERVINGS

2 ripe avocados
2 tablespoons (30 ml) lemon or lime juice
Half a small red onion, finely chopped
1 clove of garlic, crushed
2 medium tomatoes, skinned and chopped
2 tablespoons (30 ml) fresh coriander, finely chopped
Sea salt and freshly ground black pepper

To serve:
Cayenne pepper and extra virgin olive oil

Halve the avocados and scoop out the flesh. Mash the avocado flesh with the lemon or lime juice.

Add the remaining ingredients, mixing well. Alternatively, you may process the ingredients in a food processor to a coarse purée.

Check the seasoning, adding a little more black pepper or lemon juice if necessary. Chill.

Just before serving, sprinkle with a little cayenne pepper and drizzle with olive oil.

THIS AUBERGINE DIP HAS A DELICATE, SLIGHTLY NUTTY FLAVOUR AND IS EXCELLENT WITH VEGETABLE CRUDITÉS. AUBERGINES, THE BASE OF THIS DIP, ARE ULTRA-LOW IN CALORIES, RICH IN POTASSIUM AND FOLIC ACID. TAHINI IS A SESAME SEED PASTE, AVAILABLE FROM SUPERMARKETS AND HEALTH STORES.

BABA GANOUSH
MAKES 4 SERVINGS

1 medium aubergine

3 tablespoons (45 ml) lemon juice

2 tablespoons (30 ml) tahini

1 clove of garlic, crushed

Sea salt

Fresh chopped parsley to garnish

Prick the aubergine all over with a fork then place under a moderate grill, turning frequently until the skin is slightly charred. Allow to cool.

Cut in half lengthways and scrape out the softened flesh with a spoon.

Chop the flesh finely, put it in a bowl and mix with the lemon juice, tahini, garlic and salt. Garnish with the parsley and serve.

baba ganoush

CHAPTER 14
DESSERTS

CANTALOUPE MELON
IS ONE OF THE RICHEST
SOURCES OF BETACAROTENE.
ITS NATURALLY SWEET
AND AROMATIC FLAVOUR
GOES PERFECTLY WITH
THE SLIGHT TARTNESS OF
THE RASPBERRIES AND
GREEN GRAPES.

GREEN AND RED FRUIT
MAKES 4 SERVINGS

Half a cantaloupe melon

225 g (8 oz) raspberries

225 g (8 oz) seedless green grapes

200 ml (7 fl oz) apple juice

Remove the seeds from the melon. Cut the flesh into bite-sized pieces or scoop out with a melon baller.

Combine the prepared fruit and fruit juice in a bowl.

Spoon into individual bowls and serve alone or with tofu 'cream' (see recipe on page 118) if you like.

green
and red fruit

A SOUP MADE WITH STRAWBERRIES MAY SOUND UNUSUAL BUT THIS FRENCH-DERIVED VERSION IS ULTRA-SIMPLE TO MAKE AND TASTES DELICIOUS! AS IT IS NOT COOKED, THE STRAWBERRIES RETAIN ALL OF THEIR VITAMIN C.

STRAWBERRY SOUP WITH MINT
MAKES 4 SERVINGS

600 g (20 oz) fresh strawberries
400 ml (14 fl oz) cranberry and raspberry juice
About 12 fresh mint leaves, chopped

Wash the strawberries. Remove the hulls and cut the berries in half.

Put the strawberries and half of the cranberry and raspberry juice in a blender or food processor and blend until smooth.

Add the remaining juice and blend once more.

Chill well. When you are ready to serve, ladle into bowls and sprinkle with the chopped mint leaves.

strawberry soup with mint

MAKE THE MOST OF
SUMMER BERRIES WHEN
THEY ARE IN SEASON WITH
THIS STUNNING DESSERT. IT
IS EASY TO MAKE YET GOOD-
LOOKING ENOUGH TO SERVE
TO DINNER GUESTS! IT'S
MADE WITH AGAR-AGAR,
WHICH IS DERIVED FROM
SEAWEED, RATHER THAN
GELATINE (MADE FROM
COWS' HOOVES!)

SUMMER FRUITS JELLY
MAKE 4 SERVINGS

**1 heaped tablespoon (15 ml) agar-agar flakes
(or 1 sachet of powdered agar-agar)
200 ml (7 fl oz) water
400 ml (7 fl oz) cranberry and raspberry juice
(from a carton)
250 g (9 oz) of any combination of fresh strawberries,
raspberries, blackcurrants, redcurrants or blueberries
(alternatively, use frozen)**

Mix together the agar-agar and water in a small
saucepan. Bring to the boil, whisking continuously,
reduce the heat and simmer for 4–5 minutes.

Add the fruit juice and mix together. Leave to cool.

Divide the fruit between 4 glass tumblers or glass
dessert bowls and pour the cooled liquid jelly over
to cover the fruit.

Chill in the fridge until set.

summer fruits jelly

PAPAYA AND MANGO ARE
BOTH TERRIFIC SOURCES
OF BETACAROTENE
AND VITAMIN C. LIME
COMPLEMENTS BOTH
OF THEIR FLAVOURS
WONDERFULLY AND BOOSTS
THE VITAMIN C CONTENT.

PAPAYA, MANGO AND LIME SALAD
MAKES 4 SERVINGS

1 large papaya

1 large mango

2 limes

2 teaspoons (10 ml) clear acacia honey

60 g (2 oz) flaked toasted almonds

Cut the papaya in half, remove the seeds and peel.
Cut the flesh into cubes.

Slice through the mango either side of the stone.
Peel, then cut the flesh into cubes.

Place the fruit in a serving bowl.

Finely grate the rind from the limes and add to the fruit.
Squeeze the juice then put in a small saucepan with the
acacia honey. Heat gently, stirring, just until the honey
has dissolved. Allow to cool.

Pour the cooled lime juice over the fruit and toss well.
Sprinkle over the flaked toasted almonds and serve.

papaya, mango
and lime salad

RHUBARB IS VERY LOW IN CALORIES, HIGH IN FIBRE AND THE YOUNG PINK STALKS ALSO CONTAIN VITAMIN C. IN THIS RECIPE, ITS SHARP TASTE IS BALANCED PERFECTLY BY SWEET-TASTING STRAWBERRIES. MAKE A LARGER BATCH WHEN RHUBARB IS IN SEASON TO FREEZE AND USE LATER FOR CRUMBLES.

RHUBARB AND STRAWBERRY COMPOTE
MAKES 4 SERVINGS

225 g (8 oz) rhubarb stalks, trimmed and chopped

225 g (8 oz) strawberries, hulled and halved

1 tablespoon (15 ml) clear honey

125 ml (4 fl oz) orange juice

1–2 teaspoons (5–10 ml) ground ginger

Mint leaves to decorate

Put the rhubarb, strawberries, honey, orange juice and ginger in a saucepan. Stir and bring to the boil. Reduce the heat and simmer for 8 minutes until the fruit is just tender.

Allow to cool.

Spoon the fruit mixture into four serving dishes. Decorate with mint leaves.

rhubarb and strawberry compote

GRILLED FRUIT KEBABS
WITH HONEY GLAZE

MAKES 4 SERVINGS

225 g (8 oz) fresh pineapple

12 strawberries

1 mango

2 firm bananas

2 tablespoons (30 ml) lemon juice

Glaze:

3 tablespoons (45 ml) clear honey

Zest and juice of 1 orange

1/4 teaspoon ground clove

THESE FRUIT KEBABS
MAKE A STUNNING
DESSERT. MANGOES
ARE PACKED WITH
BETACAROTENE AND
THEIR FLAVOUR
COMPLEMENTS THE
SWEETNESS OF THE
PINEAPPLE AND
STRAWBERRIES.

Peel the pineapple and cut into chunks. Leave the strawberries whole with the hulls on.

Slice through the mango either side of the stone. Peel, then cut the flesh into large chunks. Peel the bananas and cut into 2.5 cm (1 in) slices. Sprinkle with a little lemon juice to prevent them turning brown.

Thread the fruit onto 4 wooden skewers, making sure that each has a mixture of fruit, and place in a large shallow dish.

To make the glaze, mix together the honey, orange zest and juice and ground cloves and pour over the kebabs. Cover and marinate for 30 minutes, turning once.

Place the fruit skewers under a hot grill or on a barbecue and cook them for 5–6 minutes, turning frequently, until the fruit is hot.

grilled fruit kebabs
with honey glaze

THIS RECIPE IS A DELICIOUS WAY OF USING SUMMER BERRIES. AS THEY ARE NATURALLY SWEET, THERE'S NO NEED TO ADD EXTRA SUGAR. THE TOPPING INCLUDES OATS, WHICH ARE RICH IN SOLUBLE FIBRE AND MINERALS, AND ALMONDS, WHICH ALSO SUPPLY PROTEIN.

SUMMER FRUITS CRUMBLE
MAKES 4 SERVINGS

300 g (10 oz) summer fruits, e.g. raspberries, blackcurrants, strawberries, blueberries, redcurrants, cherries (stoned)
2 tablespoons (30 ml) water
2 tablespoons (30 ml) clear honey
60 g (2 oz) flaked almonds, crushed
60 g (2 oz) oats
25 g (1 oz) millet flakes
25 g (1 oz) rice flour
60 g (2 oz) dairy-free spread

Pre-heat the oven to 190 C/ 375 F/ Gas mark 5.

Put the prepared fruit into an ovenproof dish. In a saucepan, melt 1 tablespoon (15 ml) of the honey with the water over a low heat. Pour over the fruit and mix together.

Place the flaked almonds, oats, millet flakes, rice flour, dairy-free spread and the remaining honey in a bowl and mix together with your fingers until you have a sticky crumb mixture. Alternatively, put in a food processor and pulse until the mixture forms fine crumbs.

Spread the oat crumble over the fruit and bake in the oven for about 25 minutes until the topping is golden.

STRAWBERRY MOUSSE

MAKES 4 SERVINGS

450 g (1 lb) ripe strawberries

300 g (10 oz) silken tofu

Grated zest of 1 orange

SUPER-RICH IN VITAMIN C, STRAWBERRIES ALSO CONTAIN ELLAGIC ACID, A POWERFUL CANCER-FIGHTING COMPOUND. IN THIS RECIPE, THEY ARE COMBINED WITH TOFU, AN EXCELLENT SOURCE OF HIGH-QUALITY PROTEIN AND CALCIUM. THIS DESSERT CONTAINS NO ADDED SUGAR BUT, IF YOU ARE SERVING TO OTHER FAMILY MEMBERS WITH A SWEET TOOTH, YOU MAY NEED TO ADD A LITTLE HONEY OR ICING SUGAR TO THEIR PORTION.

Reserve 4 strawberries for decoration. Roughly chop the rest and place in a blender or food processor with the tofu and orange zest. Blend until smooth.

Spoon into glass dishes, decorate with the reserved strawberries and chill in the fridge.

strawberry mousse

THIS DELICIOUS EASY-
TO-MAKE DESSERT IS A
TERRIFIC WAY OF USING
PEACHES WHEN THEY ARE
PLENTIFUL AND CHEAP. THEY
ARE RICH IN VITAMIN C – ONE
PEACH PROVIDES HALF OF
YOUR DAILY NEEDS – AND
POTASSIUM, GOOD FOR
REDUCING WATER
RETENTION.

PEACH AND RASPBERRY FOOL

MAKES 4 SERVINGS

4 ripe peaches

225 g (8 oz) raspberries

300 g (10 oz) silken tofu

1 teaspoon (5 ml) vanilla extract

1 tablespoon (15 ml) clear honey (optional)

A few extra raspberries

Remove the skin* and stone from the peaches and
roughly chop the flesh. Place in a blender or food
processor with the raspberries, tofu, vanilla extract
and honey (if using).

Blend until smooth.

Decorate with a few raspberries. Chill in the fridge
and serve.

* To remove the skin, plunge the peaches into a bowl
of boiling water for 30 seconds. The skin should loosen
enough for you to remove it using a sharp knife.

peach and
raspberry fool

THIS DESSERT IS ULTRA-SIMPLE TO MAKE AND AN EXCELLENT FAT-FREE ALTERNATIVE TO DAIRY ICE CREAM. BANANAS PROVIDE POTASSIUM, FIBRE, VITAMIN C AND VITAMIN B6.

BANANA AND VANILLA ICE
MAKES 4 SERVINGS

4 ripe bananas
1 teaspoon (5 ml) vanilla extract

Break the bananas into chunks. Transfer to a small plastic container.

Cover and place in the freezer for several hours.

When you are ready to serve the dessert, place the frozen banana chunks in a food processor with the vanilla extract and blend for 2–3 minutes until smooth and creamy.

Serve immediately in individual bowls.

banana and vanilla ice

UNLIKE SHOP-BOUGHT VARIETIES, THIS DELICIOUS SORBET IS MADE ENTIRELY FROM NATURAL INGREDIENTS AND CONTAINS NO ADDED SUGAR OR ARTIFICIAL ADDITIVES.

MANGO ICE
MAKES 4 SERVINGS

2 ripe mangoes

Slice through the mango either side of the stone. Peel, then cut the flesh into cubes. Place in a covered container and freeze for several hours.

When you are ready to serve it, place the frozen mango cubes in a food processor and blend for 2–3 minutes until smooth.

Serve immediately.

USE THIS DELICIOUS
LOW-FAT TOPPING AS A
SUBSTITUTE FOR CREAM
ON FRESH FRUIT DESSERTS.

TOFU 'CREAM'

300 g (10 oz) silken tofu, drained

Juice and zest of 1 orange

1 teaspoon (5 ml) lemon juice

2 teaspoons (10 ml) clear honey, optional

Place all of the ingredients in a blender or food
processor, adding a little honey to taste, if necessary.
Process until smooth and creamy. Cover and chill
in the fridge until needed.

tofu
cream

CHAPTER 15
JUICES AND SMOOTHIES

How to juice

A citrus juicer is ideal for extracting the juice from lemons, oranges, limes and grapefruit,

but for other fruit and vegetables you will need a juice extractor. They work by separating the fruit or vegetable juice from the pulp. You generally get what you pay for, so if you are serious about juicing it is worth investing in the best machine that you can afford. Choose a juicer with a reputable brand name that has an opening big enough for larger fruit and vegetables, and make sure that it is easy to clean.

There are two main mechanisms for juicers: centrifugal and masticating. Centrifugal juicers are the most popular and relatively inexpensive. The fruit and vegetables are fed into a spinning grater and the pulp is separated from the juice by centrifugal force. The pulp is retained in the machine and the juice runs into a separate jug. Masticating juicers work by mashing the fruit and vegetables and pushing them through a fine mesh. They are more expensive, but produce more juice then centrifugal juicers.

Prepare the ingredients for juicing just before juicing so they won't lose their vitamins. Cut fruit and vegetables into manageable pieces. You can put most parts of the produce into the juicer, except hard skins (e.g. citrus peel, banana peel, etc.) and stones (e.g. from avocados, peaches, apricots, etc.).

BOTH CARROTS AND APPLES ARE GREAT CLEANSERS. CARROTS ARE SUPER-RICH IN BETACAROTENE, WHILE APPLES CONTAIN QUERCETIN, A POTENT ANTIOXIDANT THAT HAS STRONG ANTI-CANCER ACTIONS.

CLASSIC DETOX

MAKES 300 ML (1/2 PINT)

2 apples

4 carrots

Using a juice extractor, juice all the ingredients, pour into a glass and serve immediately.

PACKED WITH VITAMIN C, POTASSIUM AND ANTIOXIDANTS, THIS DELICIOUS JUICE IS A TERRIFIC WAY OF GETTING ALL THE GOODNESS OF SUMMER FRUITS. IT'LL ALSO RE-ENERGISE YOU.

SUMMER BERRY DETOX

MAKES 200 ML (7 FL OZ)

1 kiwi fruit

6 strawberries

60 g (2 oz) raspberries

175 g (6 oz) pineapple

Using a juice extractor, juice all the ingredients, pour into a glass and serve immediately.

summer berry

SPRING CLEAN

MAKES 200 ML (7 FL OZ)

2 carrots

125 g (4 oz) cabbage

60 g (2 oz) celery

25 g (1 oz) watercress

Using a juice extractor, juice all the ingredients, pour into a glass and serve immediately.

CABBAGE IS A GREAT DETOXIFIER. IT CONTAINS COMPOUNDS THAT HELP THE LIVER FUNCTION PROPERLY AS WELL AS PROTECTING AGAINST CANCER. CELERY, WATERCRESS AND CARROTS ARE GOOD ACCOMPANIMENTS AS THEY ARE POWERFUL INTESTINAL CLEANSERS.

spring clean

WATERMELON REVIVER

MAKES 300 ML (½ PINT)

**A quarter of a watermelon
(about 300 g/ 10 oz flesh)
1 orange, peeled
125 g (4 oz) raspberries**

Using a juice extractor, juice all the ingredients,
pour into a glass and serve immediately.

WATERMELON IS A GREAT DIURETIC, SPEEDING THE PASSAGE OF FLUIDS CARRYING TOXINS THROUGH THE SYSTEM. IT ALSO CONTAINS BETACAROTENE AND LYCOPENE, A POWERFUL CANCER-FIGHTING COMPOUND.

BERRY BOOSTER

MAKES 200 ML (7 FL OZ)

**125 g (4 oz) blueberries
2 apples
350 g (12 oz) blackberries**

Using a juice extractor, juice all the ingredients,
pour into a glass and serve immediately.

BLUEBERRIES CONTAIN EXTREMELY POTENT ANTIOXIDANTS AND, ALONG WITH APPLES AND BLACKBERRIES, ARE TERRIFIC SOURCES OF CANCER-FIGHTING NUTRIENTS. THEY ARE SUPER IMMUNITY BOOSTERS TOO.

berry booster

IF TRAVELLING BY PLANE, BOAT OR CAR MAKES YOU FEEL QUEASY, THEN THIS JUICE MAY BE THE PERFECT SOLUTION. GINGER IS IDEAL FOR QUELLING NAUSEA, AS WELL AS BEING A GREAT INTERNAL CLEANSER. COMBINED WITH THE DIGESTIVE BENEFITS OF APPLE AND ORANGE, IT IS IDEAL FOR DRINKING JUST BEFORE TRAVELLING.

TRAVELLER'S TONIC

MAKES 200 ML (7 FL OZ)

2 apples

1 orange

2.5 cm (1 in) fresh root ginger, roughly chopped

Using a juice extractor, juice all the ingredients, pour into a glass and serve immediately.

traveller's tonic

AFTER A LONG, COLD WINTER, YOU MAY BE LEFT FEELING LOW AND PRONE TO COLDS AND FLU. DARK GREEN LEAFY VEGETABLES, SUCH AS SPINACH, WATERCRESS AND PARSLEY, ARE RICH IN IRON AND FOLIC ACID, WHICH BUILD HEALTHY RED BLOOD CELLS. SPIRULINA IS A NATURALLY CONCENTRATED SOURCE OF THESE NUTRIENTS TOO AND WILL HELP TO GIVE YOUR IMMUNE SYSTEM AN EXTRA BOOST.

IRON BOOSTER

MAKES 200 ML (7 FL OZ)

1 handful of watercress

225 g (8 oz) spinach

25 g (1 oz) parsley

2 carrots

A quarter of a cucumber

1 teaspoon (5 ml) Spirulina (optional)

Using a juice extractor, juice all the ingredients, pour into a glass and serve immediately.

VITAMIN-C-RICH SUMMER FRUITS WILL BOOST YOUR ENERGY AND NUTRIENT LEVELS. THE LINSEEDS IN THIS DRINK ARE RICH IN HEART-HEALTHY OMEGA-3 OILS AND ARE, THEMSELVES, POWERFUL INTESTINAL CLEANSERS.

ENERGISER
MAKES 200 ML (7 FL OZ)

225 g (8 oz) strawberries

1 kiwi fruit

1 apple

1 tablespoon (15 ml) linseeds (ground)

Using a juice extractor, juice all the ingredients, pour into a glass and serve immediately.

energiser

SUPER-CHARGE

MAKES 300 ML (½ PINT)

A quarter of a pineapple (about 200 g/ 7 oz flesh)

A quarter of a galia melon (about 200 g/ 7 oz flesh)

1 mango, peeled and stoned

Handful of seedless green grapes

Using a juice extractor, juice all the ingredients,
pour into a glass and serve immediately.

THIS DRINK IS
EXCELLENT FOR
BOOSTING YOUR
ENERGY AND VITALITY.
THE NATURAL FRUIT
SUGARS HELP TO
BALANCE YOUR BLOOD-
SUGAR LEVELS AND
PROVIDE YOUR BODY
WITH FUEL. IT IS ALSO
A GREAT SOURCE
OF VITAMIN C,
BETACAROTENE,
POTASSIUM AND
MAGNESIUM.

super-
charge

THIS JUICE IS HIGH IN
VITAMIN C AND MAGNESIUM,
WHICH ARE NEEDED FOR
THE HEALTHY FUNCTIONING
OF THE ADRENAL GLANDS.
IF YOU HAVE BEEN GOING
THROUGH A STRESSFUL
PERIOD LATELY AND
FEEL A BIT BELOW PAR,
THIS DRINK WILL HELP
REPLENISH YOUR DEPLETED
NUTRIENT LEVELS.

STRESS BUSTER
MAKES 200 ML (7 FL OZ)

A quarter of a cucumber

125 g (4 oz) strawberries

2 slices cantaloupe melon

1 kiwi fruit

Using a juice extractor, juice all the ingredients,
pour into a glass and serve immediately.

stress buster

smoothies

How to make smoothies

Smoothies are made from whole pulverised soft-textured fruit, such as strawberries or bananas, blended with fruit juice, yoghurt or milk. All you need is a blender or food processor. And, if you are keen, you may wish to invest in a smoothie maker, which has a dispensing tap for easy pouring and a stirrer.

For best results, choose ripe fruit and remove thick peel (e.g. from bananas), stones (e.g. from cherries or peaches) and hulls (e.g. from strawberries). Cut the flesh into large chunks. If your blender crushes ice (not all models do this), start with ice cubes blended to a 'snow' followed by the fruit. Otherwise, put ice cubes in the serving glass, blend the ingredients then pour over the ice cubes.

THIS VITAMIN-C-PACKED DRINK WILL BOOST YOUR ENERGY AND IMMUNITY. RASPBERRIES CONTAIN POWERFUL ANTI-CANCER ANTIOXIDANTS.

RASPBERRY AND ORANGE SMOOTHIE

MAKES 2 DRINKS

225 g (8 oz) raspberries

150 ml (5 fl oz) carton plain soya yoghurt

300 ml (1/2 pint) orange juice

Place the raspberries and yoghurt in a smoothie maker, blender or food processor, and process until smooth and creamy.

Add the orange juice and process for a further 30 seconds or until well combined. Serve immediately.

raspberry and orange

STRAWBERRY AND MANGO SMOOTHIE

MAKES 2 DRINKS

About 12 strawberries

1 ripe mango, peeled, stone removed, and chopped

Grated zest and juice of 1 lime

About 10 ice cubes

Put the strawberries, mango, lime zest and juice and ice cubes in the goblet of a smoothie maker, blender or food processor and process until smooth. Add a little water if you want a thinner consistency.

THIS DELICIOUS COMBINATION OF SUMMER FRUITS IS BURSTING WITH VITAMIN C AND BETACAROTENE.

strawberry and mango

APRICOTS AND NECTARINES ARE HIGH IN BETACAROTENE, FIBRE AND OTHER PHYTONUTRIENTS THAT PROTECT THE BODY FROM HEART DISEASE AND CANCER.

SUMMER FRUIT SMOOTHIE
MAKES 2 DRINKS

2 ripe nectarines

2 ripe apricots

85 g (3 oz) raspberries

About 10 ice cubes

Remove the stones from the fruit. Place the fruit in the goblet of a smoothie maker, blender or food processor; add the ice cubes and a little water. Process until smooth.

summer fruit

COCONUT MILK IS VERY LOW IN CALORIES AND VIRTUALLY FAT-FREE. AVOID THE SWEETENED VARIETY THAT COMES IN CANS, AS IT IS FULL OF SUGAR AND HIGH IN FAT. HERE IT IS BLENDED WITH MANGO, RICH IN BETACAROTENE, BUT YOU MAY USE OTHER FRUIT SUCH AS PEACHES, APRICOTS OR PAPAYA.

COCONUT AND MANGO SMOOTHIE
MAKES 2 DRINKS

6–10 ice cubes

1 mango, skinned, stone removed, and chopped

250 ml (8 fl oz) coconut milk

A few drops of vanilla extract

Put the ice cubes in the goblet of a smoothie maker, blender or food processor and process until slushy. Add the mango, coconut milk and vanilla and blend until smooth. Serve immediately.

coconut and mango

THIS MIXTURE OF SUMMER FRUIT IS BURSTING WITH VITAMIN C, BETACAROTENE AND OTHER POTENT ANTIOXIDANTS. IT WILL BOOST YOUR ENERGY LEVELS AND UPLIFT YOUR MOOD.

TROPICAL FRUIT SMOOTHIE

MAKES 2 DRINKS

About 10 ice cubes

Juice and zest of 1 lime

125 g (4 oz) strawberries

125 g (4 oz) fresh pineapple

Half a mango, peeled and roughly chopped

A quarter of a galia melon, peeled and chopped

1 banana, peeled and roughly chopped

Place the ice cubes in the goblet of a smoothie maker, blender or food processor and process until slushy.

Add the remaining ingredients, in batches if necessary, and blend until smooth. Serve in chilled glasses immediately.

tropical fruit

PACKED WITH VITAMIN C, POTASSIUM AND FIBRE, THIS SMOOTHIE WILL ENERGISE YOU. YOU COULD ALSO ADD A TEASPOON OF BLUE-GREEN ALGAE POWDER FOR EXTRA VITAMINS AND MINERALS.

ORANGE, PINEAPPLE AND BANANA SMOOTHIE
MAKES 2 DRINKS

200 ml (7 fl oz) orange juice

200 g (7 oz) fresh pineapple, cut into pieces

2 bananas cut into chunks

A few ice cubes

Place the ice cubes in the goblet of a smoothie maker, blender or food processor and process until slushy.

Add the orange juice, pineapple and banana and then process for about 45 seconds until smooth. Serve immediately.

orange, pineapple and banana

ALL BERRIES ARE
TERRIFIC SOURCES OF
VITAMIN C. STRAWBERRIES
ARE ONE OF THE BEST;
JUST SEVEN GIVE YOU
YOUR DAILY REQUIREMENT
(60 MG). THEY ALSO
CONTAIN ELLAGIC ACID,
A PHYTONUTRIENT
THAT FIGHTS CANCER.

STRAWBERRY AND RASPBERRY SMOOTHIE

MAKES 2 DRINKS

About 14 strawberries

About 20 raspberries

1 banana

200 ml (7 fl oz) orange juice

About 10 ice cubes

Place the ice cubes in the goblet of a smoothie maker, blender or food processor and process until slushy.

Add the berries and banana and blend until smooth. Serve immediately.

strawberry
and raspberry

TOFU IS A TERRIFIC SOURCE OF PROTEIN AND CALCIUM. IT CAN BE USED IN PLACE OF MILK OR YOGHURT IN SMOOTHIE RECIPES TO MAKE THICK NUTRITIOUS SHAKES.

BANANA TOFU SHAKE

MAKES 2 DRINKS

150 g (5 oz) silken tofu

2 bananas, peeled and roughly chopped

400 ml (16 fl oz) apple juice

2 teaspoons linseeds, ground in a coffee grinder (optional)

About 10 ice cubes

Break up the tofu into pieces and put them into a smoothie maker, blender or food processor, along with the bananas and half of the apple juice. Blend until smooth.

Add the ground linseeds, remaining fruit juice and ice cubes and blend until smooth. Serve immediately.

banana tofu shake

RASPBERRIES ARE
SUPER-RICH IN VITAMIN C
AND POWERFUL CANCER-
PROTECTIVE COMPOUNDS.
HERE THEY ARE BLENDED
WITH SOYA MILK
(ALTERNATIVELY, YOU
MAY USE ALMOND, RICE
OR OAT MILK IF YOU
PREFER), WHICH PROVIDES
ADDED PROTEIN AND
CALCIUM. A DAILY SOY
INTAKE HAS BEEN SHOWN
TO HELP PROTECT AGAINST
BREAST CANCER.

RASPBERRY AND SOYA SHAKE
MAKES 2 DRINKS

150 g (5 oz) raspberries
450 ml (3/4 pint) soya milk
A handful of ice cubes

Put the raspberries, soya milk and ice cubes into
a smoothie maker, blender or food processor and
blend until smooth. Serve immediately.

raspberry and
soya shake

FEELING LOW? THIS ENERGISING DRINK WILL REPLENISH YOUR NUTRIENT LEVELS AND GET YOU BACK TO FULL HEALTH. BLUEBERRIES ARE TERRIFIC SOURCES OF IMMUNITY-BOOSTING VITAMIN C AND ANTIOXIDANTS CALLED ANTHOCYANINS. THE TOFU OR YOGHURT PROVIDES BODY-BUILDING PROTEIN, CALCIUM AND B VITAMINS.

POWER PUNCH
MAKES 2 DRINKS

125 g (4 oz) blueberries

1 peach, stone removed, chopped

200 ml (7 fl oz) apple juice

150 ml (5 fl oz) soya yoghurt or silken tofu

8–10 ice cubes

Put the blueberries, peaches, apple juice, yoghurt and ice cubes into a smoothie maker, blender or food processor and blend until smooth. Serve immediately.

power punch

CHAPTER 16

SUPER FOODS A–Z

This guide shows you, at a glance, which beneficial nutrients your favourite foods contain. It also gives a brief outline of the health benefits associated with each of them

Food	Rich in	Key benefits
Almonds	Protein, calcium, zinc, vitamin E, iron, magnesium	Anti-cancer effects, reduces heart disease risk, bone health
Apples	Potassium, pectin (fibre), vitamin C, quercetin (an antioxidant)	Anti-cancer effects, protect against stroke, improves bowel function
Apricots	Betacarotene, iron, potassium, soluble fibre, vitamin C	Prevent tiredness and anaemia, alleviate constipation; lower cholesterol levels
Avocados	Vitamin E, alphacarotene, vitamin B6, folic acid, vitamin C, monounsaturated fat	Heart health, lower cholesterol levels, healthy skin, good circulation
Bananas	Magnesium, potassium, vitamin B6, fibre	Good energy-boosting snack, blood pressure control, bowel health, improve mood
Bean sprouts	Vitamin C, iron, fibre, coumestrol (phytonutrients)	Fight free radicals, anti-inflammatory effects (reduce arthritis), reduce menopausal symptoms, anti-cancer effects
Beans	Protein, soluble fibre, B vitamins, iron, zinc, magnesium, calcium, plant sterols	Slow-release energy, lower cholesterol levels, control blood pressure
Blackberries, blackcurrants, blueberries	Vitamin C, anthocyanins (antioxidants), salicylates (anti-inflammatory phytonutrients), vitamin E	Anti-cancer effects, boost immunity, anti-ageing, anti-inflammatory, anti-bacterial, strengthens blood capillaries
Brazil nuts	Protein, selenium, vitamin E, magnesium, iron	Anti-cancer effects, reduce heart disease risk
Broccoli	Vitamin C, folic acid, sulphoramine (a phytonutrient), betacarotene	Anti-cancer effects (especially of the bowel, stomach, breast, lungs and kidney)
Cabbage	Vitamin C, folic acid, glucosinolates (antioxidants), betacarotene	Anti-cancer effects, liver function, general detoxification
Carrots	Betacarotene, potassium, fibre	Anti-cancer effects (especially of the lungs), healthy skin and eyesight, boosts immunity
Cashew nuts	Protein, iron, magnesium, zinc, B vitamins	Anti-cancer effects, protects against heart disease
Cherries	Anthocyanins (phytonutrients), vitamin C, potassium	Anti-cancer effects (especially of the colon and stomach), anti-inflammatory
Chickpeas	Protein, fibre (including fructo-oligosaccharides), saponins (antioxidants), iron, zinc	Lower cholesterol levels, anti-cancer effects, digestive and bowel health
Cucumber	Potassium, betacarotene (in skin)	Blood pressure control, reduces water retention

Food	Rich in	Key benefits
Fennel	Potassium, natural oils (anisic acid, fenchone)	Digestive stimulant, liver detoxification
Figs	Calcium, fibre, iron, potassium	Bone health, bowel health, digestive function, anti-cancer effects
Garlic	Antioxidants (e.g. allicin)	Heart health, anti-cancer effects, antibacterial effects, reduces blood pressure
Grapes	Potassium, polyphenols (in red grape skin)	Anti-cancer effects (red grapes), reduce heart disease risk (red grapes)
Kiwi fruit	Vitamin C, potassium, chlorophyll	Anti-cancer effects, fights free radicals, immunity boosting, heart health
Lamb's lettuce, lollo rosso lettuce	Betacarotene, iron, folic acid, vitamin C, zinc, various flavanols (phytonutrients)	Anti-cancer effects, bone health, fights free radicals, good eyesight
Lemons	Vitamin C, limonene and terpenes (phytonutrients)	Anti-cancer effects, immunity boosting, cholesterol-lowering
Lentils	Protein, fibre, iron, magnesium, folic acid, isoflavones (phytoestrogens)	Bowel and digestive health, reduce menopausal symptoms, bone health, healthy red blood cells, blood sugar control
Limes	Vitamin C, limonene (phytonutrients), bioflavanoids	Immunity boosting, anti-cancer effects, anti-inflammatory
Mango	Betacarotene, vitamin C, potassium, vitamin E	Anti-cancer effects (especially of the colon and cervix), immunity-boosting
Melon	Betacarotene (especially cantaloupe melon), vitamin C, potassium	Immunity-boosting, lower blood pressure
Oats	Soluble fibre, B vitamins, magnesium, zinc, vitamin E	Lower cholesterol levels, anti-cancer effects, regulate appetite
Olives and olive oil	Monounsaturated fats, flavones (phytonutrients), vitamin E	Reduce heart disease risk, lower cholesterol levels and blood pressure, anti-ageing, protects against rheumatoid arthritis, anti-cancer effects (especially of the breast)
Oranges	Vitamin C, folic acid, limonene and phenolic acids (flavanones), pectin	Anti-cancer effects, lower cholesterol levels, immunity-boosting, anti-bacterial, healthy blood vessels
Papayas	Betacarotene, other carotenoids, vitamin C, potassium, vitamin E	Anti-cancer effects (especially of the colon and cervix), immunity-boosting

Food	Rich in	Key benefits
Peaches	Vitamin C, betacarotene, flavanoids	Anti-cancer effects, immunity-boosting
Peanuts	Monounsaturated fats, essential fats, vitamin E, magnesium, selenium	Lowers heart disease risk, anti-cancer effects, lowers cholesterol
Peppers	Vitamin C, betacarotene, betacryptoxanthin (phytonutrient)	Lowers heart disease risk, fights free radicals, anti-cancer effects (especially of the lungs and prostate), immunity-boosting
Pineapple	Vitamin C, potassium, bromelain (enzyme that breaks down protein)	Anti-inflammatory effects, stimulates digestion, alleviates joint pain and sinusitis
Plums	Betacarotene, antioxidants, fibre, potassium	Fight free radicals, anti-cancer effects (especially of the colon), stimulate digestion, bowel health
Pumpkin seeds	Omega-3 fatty acids, iron, magnesium, zinc	Lower heart disease risk, anti-cancer effects, lower cholesterol levels, anti-inflammatory effects
Raspberries	Vitamin C, ellagic acid (antioxidant), folic acid	Immunity boosting, anti-cancer effects (especially of the breast and stomach), fights free radicals, heart health
Rye and rye bread	Vitamin E, iron, zinc	Anti-cancer effects, lower heart disease risk, regulate appetite and blood sugar levels
Sesame seeds	Calcium, iron, magnesium, zinc, fibre	Anti-cancer effects (especially of the bowel), bone health, fight free radicals
Soya milk and tofu	Protein, calcium, isoflavones (phytonutrients)	Anti-cancer effects (especially of the breast and prostate), bone health, heart health, lower cholesterol levels
Spinach	Lutein (phytonutrients), iron, vitamin C, betacarotene, folic acid	Anti-cancer effects (especially of the colon), fights free radicals, bone health, protect against macular degeneration (age-related deterioration of vision)
Strawberries	Vitamin C, ellagic acid (antioxidant), folic acid	Immunity boosting, anti-cancer effects, fights free radicals, heart health
Tomatoes	Vitamin C, lycopene (antioxidant), betacarotene	Anti-cancer effects (especially of the prostate, colon and stomach), immunity-boosting, lowers heart disease risk
Walnuts	Protein, omega-3 fats, iron, magnesium, vitamin E	Protects against free radicals; protects against heart disease, anti-inflammatory
Watercress	Betacarotene, vitamin C, iron, chlorophyll	Immunity-boosting, heart health, liver detoxification

INDEX